Young AND Female

With spirit, self-confidence and humor, eight American women tell of overcoming the limited role traditionally assigned to girls.

Young AND Female

Turning Points in the Lives
of Eight American Women:
Personal accounts compiled
with introductory notes by
Pat Ross

Random House
New York

Library of Congress Cataloging in Publication Data
Ross, Pat, comp.
Young and female.
CONTENTS: Shirley MacLaine.—Shirley Chisholm.—Dorothy Day. [etc.]
Bibliography: p.
1. Women in the United States—Biography—Juvenile literature. [1. Women in the United States—Biography] I. Title.
CT3260.R63   920.72'0973 [920]   76-37417
ISBN 0-394-82392-3   ISBN 0-394-92392-8 (lib. bdg.)

Young
AND
Female

Contents

Foreword

It is not easy for a girl to make up her mind about what she's going to do with her life. Too often, other people are trying to make it up for her.

Society's expectations for girls, unfortunately, are more narrow and limited than society's expectations for boys. At home, at school and at work, girls are too rarely encouraged to explore all the options open to boys of the same age. The pressure to conform to a traditional "feminine" role leaves a girl less chance to make her own choices.

In this book, eight modern American women tell of their struggles to overcome traditional expectations while growing up. In selections from their autobiographies, they recall still relevant experiences which became turning points in their own young lives.

The young women shown in this book are as different as the choices they make. Their backgrounds range from urban pov-

erty to suburban comfort. Some are fortunate to have parents who offer strong support and trust; others break away from the rigid conformity of their families.

The fields where these women later found fulfillment vary, too, ranging from politics to sports, from the arts to public service. And while some have devoted their lives to their work, others have found satisfaction in combining a career with marriage and parenthood.

Despite their differences, these women share a distinct bond. Spirit, determination—and often a measure of good humor— enable them to realize that being female does not have to mean being second-best.

Today more and more American girls are learning to think for themselves and to make important choices—choices that will deeply affect not only their own lives but also the lives of women, men and younger people around them.

PAT ROSS

Young
AND
Female

Shirley
MacLaine

If Shirley's life had gone as her parents planned, she would
have "married an upstanding member of the community
and had two or three able-bodied children who ate Wonder
Bread eight ways." But Shirley had ideas of her own. She
had to discover her own life style—not one mapped out
for her by other people. The traditional role assigned to
girls was too cramped for her, and so she began a search
for her own sense of identity.

3

Today her activities are unusually varied—as movie star, political activist, world traveler, author, wife and mother. Her real life has been as unconventional as any movie role. She has lived among the Masai tribe in East Africa. She has visited the remote Himalayan kingdom of Bhutan, where she was caught in the midst of a revolution. And she recently became the first woman speaker in the 137-year history of the National Democratic Club.

When Shirley decided to tell about her real-life adventures, she canceled all movie plans, took a typing course and wrote her candid and exciting autobiography, *Don't Fall Off the Mountain*. In the following selection, Shirley tells how she rebelled against her overprotective father and set out, at eighteen, for New York City with high hopes of finding a life style of her own.

I was born with very weak bone structure in my ankles. Soon after I learned to walk I began having problems. My ankles turned in so far and were so weak that with the slightest misstep I would fall. So, about age three, for therapeutic reasons, Mother took me to a ballet class. There my imagination took anchor, my energy found a channel. What started as therapy became my life. And I had an outlet for expression.

For the next fifteen years the long lines of girls in sweaty black leotards, straining in unison at the steel practice bar to the beat of the tinny piano, became my challenge, my competition. I needed no urging to join them; I loved it from the beginning. Some of the young ladies were there to lose weight, some to pass the awkward years of adolescence, others to give their mothers an extra two hours at the bridge table. But a few fragile, iron-willed youngsters truly wanted to dance, and dedicated themselves to endless hours of toil, sweat, sore muscles, and repetition. I became one of these—not fragile, but iron-willed.

We moved to Arlington, Virginia, and I went to classes in a big house built on a grassy knoll across the Potomac River in Washington, D.C. The house was renovated into a dance studio and became the Washington School of the Ballet.

Every afternoon during the school week, I spent an hour and a half on the bus going to and from the school. It was run by two expert lady teachers, and it was they who molded my professional attitudes toward my work. The elder was Lisa Gardiner, who had danced with Anna Pavlova. A dignified woman with silver hair, she moved with a stately gait and bearing that reminded me somehow of Cinderella's horses. She would sit for hours telling me of her travels with the ballet, and as she talked her graceful hands floated through the air, her slender pink nails accenting her words.

"If you choose to do something, be sure to do it with your utmost," she would say to me. "And remember, expect nothing and life will be velvet."

Her partner, Mary Day, was fifteen years younger

and had tiny feet that could turn out so far they made a straight line, piercing black eyes, and a temperament that would have frightened a Cossack. She was an excellent teacher, whose demanding, harsh, and sometimes irrational perfectionism made each class an event.

These were the women I strove to please, five days a week, year after year. We were not a professional group, because none of us was paid for our performances, but no greater precision could have been asked of professionals. By the time I was twelve, I was part of what I'm sure was the best amateur ballet company in the United States.

At various times during the year, we performed ballets with the National Symphony at Constitution Hall, and for these occasions we rehearsed far into the night, after our regular classes. *Cinderella, The Nutcracker, The Wizard of Oz, Hansel and Gretel.* I always played Hansel—and every other boy's role, for that matter—because I was always the tallest in the class.

Rehearsals ended at midnight. I would rush for the bus, which, it seemed, was always either late or early, but never on schedule. I'd stumble groggily from the bus an hour and a half later, and make my way down the quiet street to a dark and silent house. My dinner usually was saltine crackers smothered in ketchup and Tabasco, and with them a quart of ginger ale. I always ate standing up, and then I'd stagger to bed, rarely before two o'clock. Not surprisingly, my snacks produced nightmares, and the nightmares were always the same: night after night I missed the bus.

At six-thirty I was up again for school, ready to start over—day . . . after day . . . after day, until I was about seventeen. Rebellious, mischievous days with my brother Warren were over. I had found a way out, a destiny I could follow, a life I could make for myself so I wouldn't end up like every other petty, comfortable Baptist in the community.

I seldom saw my parents, and I didn't see Warren much after that, either. They were asleep when I left for school in the morning, because Washington-Lee was so crowded half the students went on early-morning shifts (six-thirty bus pickup), and generally asleep when I returned at night, because the bus trip home took $1\frac{1}{2}$ hours from the time midnight rehearsals ended.

It was a lonely life, for a teenager especially, but I had a purpose—a good reason for being. And I learned something about myself that still holds true: I cannot enjoy anything unless I work hard at it.

An incident occurred when I was about sixteen that still blazes in my memory. I came home from a dancing-school rehearsal distraught because they had taken the role of Cinderella away from me for our Christmas production. Miss Day and Miss Gardiner said I had simply grown too tall, and that I looked clumsy.

I remember blurting it out in tears as I climbed the stairs to go to my room to be alone. Dad was coming down the stairs. He stopped, and with finger wagging told me that that should teach me to stop trying to do things I wasn't capable of. Wasn't this episode proof enough for me that, if I attempted to go beyond my range, I would only be crushed? Hadn't he told me many times during my life? When would I believe him? When would I understand that if I tried I would only be hurt?

It was like the time I sang "I Can't Say No" a few years before, at the entertainment assembly program. I had seen *Oklahoma* and fallen in love with the comedy character Ado Annie. I somehow felt I understood the level of her comedy. I put on a silly perky hat with a huge flower square on top and big clodhopper shoes, and when I did it at school everybody laughed—they really laughed.

But Dad said I shouldn't be lulled into thinking that theirs was reliable laughter, that a high-school assembly wasn't the world, that I didn't know how to sing, and knew nothing about performing, and just because I had been tickled and moved by Celeste Holm didn't give me the right to take such a standard example of American musical comedy and desecrate it on the stage of Washington-Lee High School. . . . I never sang after that, not even "The Star-Spangled Banner" at assembly. I was too self-conscious. I thought he must be right.

He said only people who had been taught things well and had been classically trained had the background to perform and be accepted. Naïve, raw instinct was one thing, but it couldn't compare with traditional education. Only a fool would dare spread his arms wide, exposing his heart, and say—without training— "Here I am, World, I've got something to say." Only a deadhead would believe he could get away with that, because he'd get hurt—and hurt badly.

And someone who might realize the pitfalls but say, "Up yours, World, I'm going to say it anyway," would have to be put away. Not only would he be insane— he'd be dangerous. He'd be dangerous because he was willing to be hurt.

I fell on the stairs, that December evening after rehearsal, with my father over me, berating me not only for trying to perform, but for thinking that I could dance Cinderella, and for making a conspicuous ass out of myself as a result. And I cried hard—I cried so hard that I vomited. But the vomit on the stairs didn't stop him; he went right on driving home his point, that I would only be hurt if I dared to dare.

I couldn't move. I looked over at Mother in the living room. Warren wasn't home. Mother sat quietly until finally she said, "All right, Ira, that's enough."

But Ira knew that wasn't going to be the end of it. He could see, even though I had dissolved into a little pile of protoplasm, that I would never stop daring. And he seemed to understand that ironically he, in effect, was teaching me to dare because I saw that he was such a spectacular disappointment to himself for having never tried it. A strange clear look of understanding came into his eyes as he realized I didn't want to be like him. He stepped over the vomit and went to the kitchen to fix himself a drink.

It was then that I determined to make the most of whatever equipment I had been born with, and part of that equipment was to dare. But mostly I didn't want to be a disappointment to myself.

It was the evening of the *Cinderella* performance. I was dancing the Fairy Godmother, and I stood in the wings after completing my *pliés* and warming-up exercises. The orchestra tuned up, the house lights dimmed, and the audience quieted.

The overture began and the curtain was about to open. Before it did, I took a few practice *grands jetés* across the stage. *Snap*—I went down. A sharp pain pierced my right ankle as it doubled under me. Terrified, I looked quickly around to see if anyone had noticed. No one had. Dancers fall down all the time. I looked at the ankle. It was already swollen. I tightened my toe-shoe ribbon to a death grip, and stood up. The curtain went up.

I climbed on point and began to dance. With each movement I seemed to step further out of myself. The pain left me. I began to feel a sense of triumph that gave me strength—not an anesthetized strength as though I had dulled the pain, but more as though my mind had risen above me and was looking down. The dance movements came in an easy flow, and I felt that I was soaring above myself. I knew the pain was there, but I was on top of it somehow. It was probably my first experience in mind over matter. And the feeling was exquisite. On a ballet stage in Washington, D.C., I first came in contact with my potential talent for becoming a mystic!

Two and a half hours later the ballet and curtain calls were over. I asked for an ambulance, and then the pain hit me. I didn't walk for four months.

While I was laid up with my broken ankle I asked mother to have a talk with me. There had never been many significant talks between us, because I always felt that "significant" subjects would be painful for her. But this talk was necessary, and I would have to stumble in the dark a bit, hoping that I could find part of her that I wouldn't hurt.

I remember sitting with my foot up on pillows on the edge of my bed in my room, gazing at my freckled face in a hand mirror. My face embarrassed me most of the time and I couldn't get a comb through my mass of unruly, tangled red hair.

Mother paused in front of the door. With a glance toward the back yard where my father sat, she entered the room and sat down beside me on the bed.

"What's wrong?" she asked, bracing herself as though anticipating disaster.

"I guess I want to be too many things, too many people," I began, gesturing at the walls covered with the symbols of my restlessness.

She looked at the maps, the photographs of famous ballerinas, at the books filled with other people and other places, and at the high-powered telescope I wished would take me to the moon. The familiar sad sparkle filled her eyes.

"But I have to go away from here—away from the schedule, the rigid discipline, the conformity. Perhaps it's been good, and useful, and necessary, but there's so much out there I have to see, and have to do, and have to be a part of."

My words were cutting straight through to her heart, I could see that, and her expression was more than I could bear. She understood only too well. It was something she had wanted to do herself once, a long time ago when her spirit was independent, before she succumbed to being what she thought she *should* be. Her friends told me she had been "delightfully carefree" and that her gaiety had infected everyone she met. I never remembered her that way. I wondered what had happened, and I guess I didn't want it to happen to me.

She changed her position on the bed. "The ballet is stifling you, too, isn't it?"

"Yes," I answered. "I don't know how it started or why, but ballet seems so limited. Miss Gardiner and Miss Day are always telling me not to move my face so much, but I can't help it, and I don't *want* to help it. If the music means laughter to me, my face smiles, naturally. They told me that if I can't control it I should go into movies or something."

"What do *you* want to do to express yourself?" she asked.

"I want to interpret people and what they think and feel. I think I love people, but I don't know very much about them. And I want to be more specific about the way I express myself. I don't want to be a mechanical doll in a mechanical art, and I'm not even sure I want to dance it."

"Have you thought about how you would do it?"

"Well, yes, but I never get very far because I'm afraid."

"Afraid of what?"

"Well, I don't know how to explain it. It's something about being stuck with being me."

"What do you mean?"

"Well, you know how much I love the Spanish dance, for instance."

"Yes."

"And you know that at ballet school it's my favorite class, and you know that I've worked hard at the castanets and the heel beats, and you know that Miss Gardiner and Miss Day think that I'm the best one in the class since Liane left."

"Yes," she agreed. "I think so, too."

"Well, even though it's something I really love doing, I'm self-conscious about it."

"Why?"

"Because how can I expect the audience to believe that I'm a Spanish dancer if I'm really an American girl from Virginia? How can I ever be anything more if that's what I really am?"

Mother folded her hands in her lap, sat up straighter than she had in years.

"Above all, you must know emotions. Study how people *feel*. I believe that is one thing we are all capable of understanding in others. We may not always be able to understand how they live, or accept what they eat, who they pray to, or why they die, but we can all, with a little effort, understand how another *feels*. How does a Spanish dancer feel? She dances to the same music we hear. What does she feel when she hears it? When you can convey what she feels, then anyone would believe you're a Spanish dancer, too, in spite of your red hair and freckles."

I hugged her. She didn't seem trampled on any more.

"May I go to New York? May I go as soon as I graduate?"

All her years of frustration came alive in one moment. The sad sparkle vanished from her eyes. She answered with unflinching certainty. "Yes, it's time. Your father won't like the idea, he'll think you'll get hurt or taken, but then isn't that always the risk? I think you're prepared."

So I was free to try my wings.

Shirley
Chisholm

A wiry black woman rises again and again, gesturing for permission to speak before a meeting of all the Democrats of the 91st Congress. The Congresswoman from an inner-city district of Brooklyn wants to point out the inappropriateness of her assignment to the Agriculture Committee.

But the chairman continues to ignore Shirley Chisholm, who is expected to be seen and not heard during her freshman term. Her male colleagues smirk and nudge one another as the new Congresswoman grows more determined.

Then, suddenly, the petite figure rises and walks down the long aisle to the chairman's platform. At this point it is no longer possible for him to ignore her. "I've been trying to get recognition for half an hour, Mr. Chairman," she says, "but evidently you were unable to see me. So I came down to the well." She is finally allowed to make a short speech.

Soon thereafter, Congresswoman Chisholm is transferred to the Veterans' Affairs Committee. Although this new post still seems remote from the needs of the poor in her district, she accepts it good-naturedly, saying: "There are a lot more veterans in my district than there are trees."

Shirley continues to catch Congress off guard with such frank statements and attitudes, and with her unwillingness to play the political games of what she calls "the senility system." In her first speech in Congress in 1968 she criticized the spending of vast sums for military purposes—funds which, she stated, were needed at home for social reform. More recently she has introduced bills dealing with such important issues as day care and a revision of the social-security laws to make them fairer to both sexes.

When the former Shirley St. Hill was a young woman, many people told her she had both the brains and the stamina for a political career. Two great stumbling blocks kept her from trying: she was black and she was female. Although she believed that both blacks and women needed to improve their conditions through political action, she accepted the easier road open to her at that time—teaching in a child-care center in Harlem.

Years passed before Shirley had gained enough courage and self-confidence to rock the boat and, eventually, beat the system. When she looks back on her personal struggle she states: "Of my two 'handicaps,' being female put more obstacles in my path than being black."

"Unbought and Unbossed" was Shirley Chisholm's street-corner campaign slogan. It is now the title of the auto-biography which expresses both her spirit and her confidence in future generations.

In the excerpt that follows, Shirley tells how it all began.

———————————◆———————————

I was still naive about most things when I entered college, not quite eighteen. My fiercely protective parents had given me a sheltered upbringing that was incredible, considering the time and place in which I grew up. In school, my intelligence had put me in a special category. In college, I began to bump up against more of the world.

I had already decided to become a teacher. There was no other road open to a young black woman. Law, medicine, even nursing were too expensive, and few schools would admit black men, much less a woman. Social work was not yet open to blacks in the early 1940s.

If I had other ideas about what I might do, I dismissed them. My youth may have been sheltered from boys and some other realities, but I was black, and nobody needed to draw me a diagram. No matter how well I prepared myself, society wasn't going to give me a chance to do much of anything else. (My sister Muriel, who entered Brooklyn College a few years later, majored in physics and graduated magna cum laude. She was unable to find a job, even as a laboratory technician.) I knew it would have to be teaching for me.

More and more people, white and black, began to tell me things like, "Shirley, you have potential. You should do something with your life." I felt they were right. There must be a role for me to play, but what? As a teacher, perhaps I could use the talents people were telling me about and which I felt were there to do something that would be of service to society—especially to children. I volunteered to work in an Urban League settlement house, teaching art classes and sewing, and writing and producing skits and plays, which I loved. I decided to devote my life to children.

But the resolve was also there (I did not realize yet how fierce it had grown) to do something about the way whites treated my people. Political action was hardly even a fantasy for me at that time. But I decided that if I ever had a chance, somehow I would tell the world how things were as I saw them.

A blind political science professor, Louis Warsoff, became interested in me, and we had long talks. I called him "Proffy," affectionately. He was one of the first white men whom I ever really knew and trusted. Our white neighbors and my father's co-workers had never been friends; they did not visit us and we did not visit them, and our interrelations were always a little strained even when they were at their best. From

Professor Warsoff I learned that white people were not really different from me.

I loved formal debating particularly, and once after I starred in a match he told me, "You ought to go into politics."

I was astonished at his naiveté.

"Proffy," I said, "you forget two things. I'm black— and I'm a woman."

"You really have deep feelings about that, haven't you?" he countered.

The conversation stuck in my mind. I realized that I did have deep feelings, on both scores.

Women were not even elected to campus offices then. Twice when girls ran for president of the Student Council (they were white, of course) I threw myself into the campaigns. I painted posters, helped write slogans and speeches, helped organize rallies and spoke at them myself. The white girls did not win.

I was still living at home, still going to church three times on Sundays, and still forbidden to date. I spent hours in the college library, and made no new, close friends in school. Naturally, the boys considered me a bookworm. It didn't bother me too much. They were surprised, though, when I showed up at parties and they discovered that I could dance, and loved to. No one ever had to teach me how; I just naturally danced. "That Shirley St. Hill can really move on the floor," I heard one boy say. But still the word was "Stay away from her—she's too intellectual, always talking about some big, serious thing."

During college I joined the Brooklyn chapter of the

NAACP, but I was not too active. It was primarily interested in economic issues such as discrimination in hiring, working conditions, pay, promotion. I had begun what was to be a twenty-year-long round of involvement with one community service organization after another, most of which I would eventually drop. I worked for the Urban League, I worked in hospitals, reading to old people and organizing programs to entertain them.

I am still active in a few of these groups, like the Brooklyn Home for the Aged. As for the rest, after I give an organization a fair chance to show that it is really out to do something, if it doesn't, I get angry. In the last twenty years I have sat through more meetings and discussions than I ever want to remember and have seen very little get done.

Even as an undergraduate, I was beginning to feel how useless it was for blacks to sit and talk with "the leading people" in the community, on biracial committees. It had begun to be clear that as long as we kept talking, nothing much was going to happen, and that this was what the "leading people" really wanted.

My interest in politics grew gradually. I joined the Seventeenth Assembly District Democratic Club and scored my first political success there as a cigar box decorator.

When I began going to membership meetings regularly, they put me on the card party committee. The party and raffle formed the year's big fund-raising event. They were run by the women of the club, most of them wives of members. Because I had a flair for painting and decorating, I was given as my first assignment the job of decorating cigar boxes to hold raffle tickets and money collected at each table during the evening. I went around and begged boxes from candy stores, painted them, and cut out pictures to decorate them. They were so beautiful that all the women were impressed. Definitely, I was going to be an asset to the club. From now on, they would have somebody to collect cigar boxes and decorate them.

When the committee met to discuss the progress of the raffle ticket sales and so on, I went a little beyond the role they had assigned me and began to make suggestions. One turned out to be a real troublemaker.

The club, I could see if they couldn't, was exploiting the women. It lived on the proceeds of the annual raffle and card party that the women ran; its only other income was from dues. But the men never provided a budget to run the event, and the women had to beg money here and there to buy prizes and print raffle books.

"Why should we put up with it?" I asked them. "We bring in the money. Why shouldn't they give us five hundred dollars or a thousand, some definite sum, to do it with?" I was angry, and as we talked, some of the women got angry themselves. They brought it up at a club meeting.

One, Molly, was the spokesman. As one of the male leaders, up front, was blathering compliments at the women for their efforts, Molly stood up and said, "I don't want to hear any of that. I want to hear what you're going to give us this year to run the party." She persisted, and others joined in.

The men huddled to see how they were going to handle the crisis.

Molly wouldn't quit. "All I want to know is how much you're going to give us."

I joined in: "Women are the backbone of this club, and you know it. You gentlemen are always using us. Well, we have no objection to that, as long as you support our efforts and give us some recognition."

The chairman rapped the gavel. "This meeting is out of order."

A woman in the back said, "It will stay out of order until you start to pay attention to us."

So at last, they gave us $700. The party, as it always did, brought in more than $8000.

After that the women occasionally spoke up at meetings and raised questions. The reaction of the men became "Shirley is egging them on." Sometimes that was true.

[In 1964, when Shirley decided to run for an opening in the New York State Assembly, her reason was straight and simple: "I was the best qualified nominee and I was not going to be denied because of my sex."]

Many women have given their lives to political organizations, laboring anonymously in the background while men of far less ability managed and mismanaged the public trust. These women hung back because they knew the men would not give them a chance. They knew their place and stayed in it. The amount of talent that has been lost to our country that way is appalling. I think one of my major uses is as an example to the women of our country, to show them that if a woman has ability, stamina, organizational skill, and a knowledge of the issues she can win public office. And if I can do it, how much more hope should that give to white women, who have only one handicap?

I am certain that more and more American women must become involved in politics. It could be the salvation of our nation. If there were more women in politics, it would be possible to start cleaning it up. Women I have known in government have seemed to me to be much more apt to act for the sake of a principle or moral purpose. They are not as likely as men to engage in deals, manipulations, and sharp tactics. A larger proportion of women in Congress and every other legislative body would serve as a reminder that the real purpose of politicians is to work for the people.

It is not female egotism to say that the future of mankind may very well be ours to determine. It is a fact. The warmth, gentleness, and compassion that are part of the female stereotype are positive human values, values that are becoming more and more important as the values of our world begin to shatter and fall from our grasp. The strength of Christ, Gandhi, and Martin Luther King was a strength of gentleness, understanding, and compassion, with no element of violence in it. It was, in short, a *female* strength, and that is the kind that often marks the highest type of man.

Dorothy
Day

During the Great Depression, with the help of a small volunteer staff, Dorothy Day started to publish a weekly newspaper called *The Catholic Worker*. It exposed little-known poverty and exploitation. Its editorials described the activities of the labor movement and urged clergymen to understand the needs and problems of working people.

Dorothy's personal ideals, expressed through the newspaper, soon inspired many people of all ages to join the Catholic Worker Movement for social change both within the Church and in society at large. Dorothy set up "hospitality houses" to welcome the needy. The Movement's communal farms encouraged women and men to work together in harmony and love.

Dorothy Day led the way for today's radical Catholic movement, which has challenged some of the age-old traditions of the Roman Catholic Church. Dorothy herself continues to uphold her original ideals by counseling conscientious objectors and supporting the peace movement.

Equality for women was one of the first causes that Dorothy actively supported. Her belief that women should be free to make their own choices was intertwined with her belief that *all* people should be free.

In her autobiography, *The Long Loneliness,* Dorothy tells how she joined a group of suffragists to picket the White House for equal rights. She was nineteen and already a journalist. The following episode describes that 1917 protest march and the resulting jail term.

———————————◆———————————

In Washington it was known by the press and police that the picket line that day would be unusually large. So when we left the headquarters of the women's party the park across from the White House was crowded with spectators. Many police held back the crowd and kept the road clear for the women picketers.

They started out, two by two, with colored ribbons of purple and gold across the bosoms of their dresses and banners in their hands. There was a religious flavor about the silent proceedings. To get to the White House gates one had to walk halfway around the park. There were some cheers from women and indignation from men, who wanted to know if the President did not have enough to bother him, and in wartime too!

By the time the third contingent of six women reached the gates—I was of this group—small boys were beginning to throw stones, and groups of soldiers and sailors appearing from the crowd were trying to wrest the banners from the hands of the women. The police arrived at once with a number of patrol wagons. I had to struggle for my banner too, with a red-faced young sailor, before a policeman took me by the arm and escorted me to the waiting police van. Our banners were carried, protruding from the back of the car, and we made a gay procession through the streets.

Bail had been provided for us and after our names and addresses were taken at the police station we were released. The trial was set for ten o'clock the next morning. When the thirty-five of us appeared, the judge pronounced us guilty and postponed the sentence.

Again that afternoon we picketed and again there was arrest, release on bail, trial and postponement. The tactics were then changed, and when we were arrested once more and taken to the Central Station, we refused to give bail and were put in the House of Detention for the night.

The facilities there were inadequate for so many prisoners. We had to sleep fifteen in a room meant for two, with cots cheek by jowl so that it was impossible to stir. The next morning we were all sentenced. Many of the women on receiving their sentences took the occasion to make speeches to the judge, who sat patiently though somewhat uncomfortably facing the righteous wrath of the thirty-five women.

The leader of the picketers received a sentence of six months, the older women were sentenced to fifteen days, and the rest of us to thirty days. We started our hunger strike right after receiving our sentences. The scant meal of weak coffee, oatmeal and bread was the last one we expected to have until our demands (for the rights of political prisoners) were granted or we were released.

I was too excited to worry much about food. I was to find that one of the uglinesses of jail life was its undertone of suppressed excitement and suspense. It was an ugly and a fearful suspense, not one of normal hope and expectation.

For many hours the women had to wait in a little room back of the court. This waiting, too, was part of the burden put upon us. Years later when I read Arthur Koestler's *Scum of the Earth,* he too spoke of the interminable hours of waiting experienced by prisoners who were being sent to a concentration camp.

Finally, at four o'clock, things began to happen to us. Prison wagons were brought, wagons that had only ventilators along the top and were otherwise closed.

Two of them sufficed to carry the prisoners to the jail.

When they reached that barren institution on the outskirts of the city, backed by a cemetery and surrounded by dreary bare fields, there was another long halt in the proceedings. After a low argument at the entrance (we never heard what people were saying and that too was part of the torture), the police vans were turned away and started off in another direction.

Those women who had served sentence before knew that we were being taken to the workhouse, and many stories had been told of what the prisoners had suffered at the hands of the violent keeper there, a man named Whittaker. We were all afraid.

It had been completely black in the prison vans but when we were ushered by a number of policewomen into a waiting train which rolled out of the station immediately, the lamps along the road had not yet been lit.

It was the beginning of November, and I sat with my face pressed against the glass watching the blue twilight, pierced with the black shapes of many scrawny trees. Here and there lamps glowed in farmhouse windows. In the west the sky still held the radiance of the sun which faded gradually and left one with a terrible sense of desolation and loneliness. It was sadly beautiful at that time of night. I was glad for the company of my friend Peggy, and we tried to stay near each other so that we would not be separated later.

There was more waiting after we had been driven from the railroad station to the administration building of the workhouse. A matron tried to take our names and case histories, which all of us refused to give.

We waited there in the administration building, while the matron sat behind her desk and knitted. The spokeswoman for our group was an elderly woman from a socially prominent family in Philadelphia and she had asked to see Mr. Whittaker, the super-intendent, before we were assigned to our cells. The matron paid no attention to her request but left us all standing, until of our own accord we took benches and chairs about the room. Some of the younger ones sat on the floor and leaned against the wall. We were beginning to be very tired.

It was not until ten o'clock that Mr. Whittaker, a large stout man with white hair and a red face, came storming into the room, leaving the door open on the porch, from which came the sound of the shuffling feet of many men.

Our spokeswoman got up and began to announce that we were all going on hunger strike unless our demands were met, but before she could get the first words out of her mouth, Whittaker had turned to the door and beckoned. Immediately the room was filled with men. There were two guards to every woman, and each of us was seized roughly by the arms and dragged out of the room. It seems impossible to believe, but we were not allowed to walk, were all but lifted from the floor, in the effort the men made to drag, rather than lead us to our place of confinement for the night.

The leaders were taken first. In my effort to get near Peggy I started to cross the room to join her, and was immediately seized by two guards. My instinctive impulse was to pull myself loose, to resist such handling, which only caused the men to tighten their hold on me, even to twist my arms painfully. I have no doubt but that I struggled every step of the way from the administration building to the cell block where we were being taken. It was a struggle to walk by myself, to wrest myself loose from the torture of those rough hands.

We were then hurled onto some benches and when I tried to pick myself up and again join Peggy in my blind desire to be near a friend, I was thrown to the floor. When another prisoner tried to come to my rescue, we found ourselves in the midst of a milling crowd of guards, being pummeled and pushed and kicked and dragged, so that we were scarcely conscious, in the shock of what was taking place.

The account of what they termed a riot was printed in the *New York Times* later, and the story made the event much worse than it was, though it was bad enough.

I found myself flung into a cell with one of the leaders, Lucy Byrnes, a tall red-haired schoolteacher from Brooklyn, with a calm, beautiful face. She was handcuffed to the bars of the cell, and left that way for hours. Every time she called out to the other women who had been placed up and down a corridor in a block of what we found out afterward were punishment cells, Whittaker came cursing outside the bars, threatening her with a straitjacket, a gag, everything but the whipping post and bloodhounds which we had heard were part of the setup at Occoquan.

An hour or so later, when things had quieted down, an old guard shuffled down the corridor and unlocked the handcuffs from the bars of the cell but left them on her wrists so that she had to sleep with them on. Each cell was made for one prisoner, so there was only a single bunk, a slab of wood in the corner. There were two blankets on it, and when I had unfastened her shoes and arranged the blankets, Lucy and I tried to make ourselves comfortable on the single slab.

In spite of our exhaustion, we could not sleep, but lay there talking of Conrad's novels for some time. Early the next morning Lucy was taken away to what we afterward heard was a padded cell for delirium tremens patients and I was left alone to try to sleep a good part of that first sad day.

There were no meals to break the monotony, and if the women tried to call out to one another, there were always guards on hand to silence them harshly. In the morning we were taken one by one to a washroom at the end of the hall. There was a toilet in each cell, open, and paper and flushing were supplied by the guard. It was as though one were in a zoo with open bars leading into the corridor.

There were only narrow ventilators at the top of the rear wall of the cell, which was a square stone room. The sun shone dimly through these slits for a time and

then disappeared for the rest of the day. There was
no way to tell what time it was. In the darkness of
the night before we had not noticed a straw mattress
in another corner of the cell. I put this on the built-in
bunk. The place was inadequately heated by one pipe
which ran along a wall. Suspense and fear kept one
cold.

It was not until the next day that we were offered
food. Then milk and toast were brought and left in
the cells for an hour, but none of our group ate. Food
was again brought that night. It was not stale toast
and cold milk, but hot milk and fragrant toast that
came to tantalize us for the next ten days.

Every now and then the women called out to each
other. We had neither pencil nor paper so we could
not write; no books, so we could not read. I found a
nail file which I began automatically to use on my nails,
and as though I had been spied on, a guard immediately
came in and took it from me.

We had no idea how many were in the punishment
block but estimated there could be no more than
twelve since there were only so many single cells. The
older women had been taken elsewhere.

"Keep the strike," one of the girls called out once.
"Remember, if it's broken we go back to worms in the
oatmeal, and the workshop."

Personally I would have preferred the workshop and
prison clothes to the hunger strike. Those first six days
of inactivity were as six thousand years. To lie there
through the long day, to feel the nausea and emptiness

of hunger, the dazedness at the beginning and the feverish mental activity that came after.

I lost all consciousness of any cause. I had no sense of being a radical, making protest against a government, carrying on a nonviolent revolution. I could only feel darkness and desolation all around me. The bar of gold which the sun left on the ceiling every morning for a short hour taunted me; and late in the afternoon when the cells were dim and the lights in the corridor were not yet lit, a heartbreaking conviction of the ugliness, the futility of life came over me so that I could not weep but only lie there in blank misery.

I lost all feeling of my own identity. I reflected on the desolation of poverty, of destitution, of sickness and sin. That I would be free after thirty days meant nothing to me. I would never be free again, never free when I knew that behind bars all over the world there were women and men, young girls and boys, suffering constraint, punishment, isolation and hardship for crimes of which all of us were guilty.

The mother who had murdered her child, the drug addict—who were the mad and who the sane? Why were prostitutes prosecuted in some cases and in others respected and fawned on? People sold themselves for jobs, for the pay check, and if they only received a high enough price, they were honored. If their cheating, their theft, their lie, were of colossal proportions, if it were successful, they met with praise, not blame. Why were some caught, not others? Why were some termed criminals and others good businessmen? What

was right and wrong? What was good and evil? I lay
there in utter confusion and misery. . . .

The hunger strike lasted for ten days. After six days
we were placed in hospital cells where there was light
and warmth. My small room then was next to Peggy's,
and the radiator which warmed my room ran through
the wooden partition so that we could pass notes, written on toilet paper with a stub of pencil which Peggy
somehow managed to keep when everything else was
taken from us.

On the other side one of the older women lay in
silence all through the day. Twice a day orderlies came
to the room. Holding her down on the bed, they forced
tubes down her throat or nose and gave her egg and
milk. It was unutterably horrible to hear her struggles,
and the rest of us lay there in our cubicles tense with
fear.

Peggy weakened on the eighth day, and took the
milk toast which was brought in to us still. She urged
me to keep her company, and I refused.

"Don't be a fool," she whispered through the aper-
ture by the radiator. "Take this crust then and suck
on it. It's better than nothing."

I accepted this compromise, and she carefully tore
off the crust of the bread and stretched it out to me.
I was just able, thanks to her long fingers and my own,
to reach it and draw it in. With what intense sensual
enjoyment I lay there in my cot, taking that crust
crumb by crumb.

I did not feel guilty for breaking the strike in this

way after eight days. All but two or three of the suffragists were holding fast and worrying the State Department, the President, the great newspaper public, besides the jail authorities. I upheld Peggy, my friend, by sharing her crust, for which I was deeply grateful, and I continued the protest we had undertaken. Cheating the prison authorities was quite in order, I reasoned.

On the tenth day the strike was broken by the announcement that all our demands would be granted, and that we would be transferred to the City Jail to which we had been sentenced.

Emily
Hahn

"You girls alone?" Emily and her friend Jane became tired of that question, even though it *was* unusual in 1924 for two young women to be traveling cross-country in a Model T Ford. Before they left, Emily's boy friend kept insisting it was not right for a *girl* to go traveling around. It was different, he added, for a *man*. Now almost everyone they met along the way seemed to express the same disapproval.

They had managed to cope with breakdowns, boiling

radiators and other disasters, so why all the fuss? "I want to get around. I want to see things," Emily insisted. And she did just that.

Emily has spent much of her life traveling. She was never content to merely pay a visit to places such as Africa, Japan and China. Instead, she settled down, adopted the local customs and tried to understand people whose ways differed from her own. She was a daring traveler and her experiences were often unique. These experiences inspired Emily to become an author. Her many books include *China to Me, England to Me* and *Animal Gardens.*

In her memoirs, *Times and Places,* Emily relates many instances when she opened doors which were clearly and unfairly labeled "For Men Only." In the following chapter from this book, she tells about her encounters with sex discrimination in engineering school.

After graduating with a degree in mining engineering, Emily found herself pigeonholed as a file clerk for mining documents—a standard dead-end job of the sort often given to women engineers. She soon ended this frustrating career, and began traveling and writing.

Although some of the prejudices Emily confronted have now been eliminated, others unfortunately remain. Women today are admitted more freely to professional schools. But they still face the frequent prospects of lower salaries and less challenging jobs than those offered to men.

My career as a mining engineer has this much in common with many success stories—it was founded on an accident. Otherwise, there is no comparison, because mine is not a success story. As an engineer, I have been a flop, but there were a few glorious weeks, back in 1926, when it might have been otherwise. Flushed with the glory and the triumph of my B.Sc., excited by the publicity which I received as the First Woman Graduate in Mining Engineering from the University of Wisconsin, and generally on top of the world, I completely forgot the reason for my acquiring that extraordinary diploma and actually took a job with a mining company. Yet the facts are simple and stark. I never meant to be a mining engineer at all. The whole thing was a complete misapprehension.

At the age of seventeen, I was an earnest, plump young woman, much annoyed by my parents' insistence on my going to college, because I felt that I was destined for Art. Once installed at the University of Wisconsin, though, I had to study something. At first I enrolled myself in the College of Letters and Science, where by temperament I belonged; it offered that potpourri of language, literature, history, and science that made, I thought, for Culture.

It was the required science course which led me astray. A half-year term of freshman geology stirred me up to try chemistry. I had heard that among the chemistry professors at Wisconsin there was a really good teacher, Kahlenberg, but when I tried to get into his class, I ran into a trifling technical difficulty. Kahlenberg's course, the dean explained, though it exactly paralleled that of the Letters and Science brand of chemistry, was usually taken only by engineering students.

"Well, that's all right," I said. "I'm sure I can persuade Professor Kahlenberg to give me special permission to go to his lectures. Since they cover the same ground, what's the difference? May I do it that way?"

Now, the dean may have fought with his wife that morning, or maybe he was worried about his bank account, or perhaps it was necessary that he say no once in a while, just to prove he was a dean. I'm sure that he never intended thus carelessly to mold my future life with one hasty word, but that is what he did. "No," said the dean rudely, and turned back to his desk.

His manners hurt my feelings, but that alone wouldn't have done the mischief. Like many young people in my day, I was bristling with principles, eager to find abuses in the world and burning to do away with them. In five seconds I had condemned the dean's decision as an abuse. He was wrong in saying no—wrong on technical grounds, because Professor Kahlenberg's consent would have been enough for any dean in a reasonable mood, and wrong in principle, because a student should be allowed to select his own teachers. Anyway, those were my sentiments.

I was mad. Boy, was I mad! I couldn't have remained in the same college with that dean for one single day more. Before the registrar's office closed that afternoon, I had transferred myself to the College of Engineering, enrolled for the chemistry course I wanted, and sent off a confused letter of explanation to my parents.

There, if only anybody in the Engineering College had had a grain of sense, the great revolt would have ended. I would have listened to Kahlenberg's chemistry lectures, shaken hands with him, and transferred myself right back to Culture and a chastened dean at the end of term. The engineers, however, were not wise.

They were stunned when they discovered me, a seventeen-year-old female freshman, enrolled in the Engineering College. The university had a long-standing tradition, as well as a charter, for being a coeducational institution. Women studied medicine at Wisconsin, and the "pure science" courses were full of girls; the Agricultural College, too, had them. Nobody argued about that. But nobody had yet heard of a coed engineer.

The engineers' immunity through the years had bred in their ranks a happy confidence that it could never happen there, and I was a horrid surprise. They lost their heads and went into a panic and, in the ensuing weeks, actually appealed to the state legislature to heave me out. After due consideration, the legislature regretfully refused. It couldn't heave me out, it explained, much as it would like to as a group of red-blooded he-men, because the university was a coeducational, tax-supported institution, and if a woman wanted to study any course it offered, and if she fulfilled the requirements and behaved herself, you couldn't turn her down.

Even then, if the engineers had only known, all was not lost. They couldn't keep their mouths shut, though. They were the engineers—hearty, simple folk. All of them, faculty members and students, tried to live up to the college pattern—the awkward guy, the diamond in the rough. To a man, they wore stiff corduroy trousers, smoked pipes or chewed tobacco, and looked down haughtily on the other colleges, which they condemned as highbrow. It was not in them to be diplomatic, and I maintain that they brought upon themselves what followed.

The custom in college is to allocate each student to a professor, who acts as his adviser. In the College of Letters and Science, my adviser had been a fragile lady who taught French literature, but my new adviser in the Engineering College was a mining engineer. I had elected mining engineering as my particular course. Professor Shorey was no pedant, nor was he tactful. My first advisory hour with him was given over to a violent argument.

"But why?" he demanded. "Why should a woman want to be an engineer? I never heard of such nonsense!"

"Why did *you* want to be an engineer?" I retorted. I was still talking in a more or less academic spirit, of course. I meant to leave engineering in peace, and before long. Sooner or later I intended to break down and explain the circumstances to Professor Shorey and

reassure him, but in the meantime his attitude interested me. I wanted to hear more about it.

"It's not at all the same thing," he said. "In the first
place, you'll never get a job, even if you should take
your degree, which is very doubtful. If I were running
a mine, I'd never hire a woman in any technical capac-
ity. You wouldn't have the practical experience, and
you'd be a nuisance around the office."

"Why wouldn't I have the experience, Mr. Shorey?"

"How would you get it? Who's going to let *you* go
down a mine? Why, the miners would go on strike.
They'd call it bad luck and expect a cave-in. It's too
foolish to discuss. It's all a waste of time, anyhow—your
time and mine—because you won't get your degree."

I moved closer to the desk, all alert. "Why won't
I get my degree?" I said.

Shorey sighed. "The female mind," he explained
carefully and kindly, "is incapable of grasping mechanics or higher mathematics or any of the funda-
mentals of mining taught in this course."

That remark, *tout simple*, is why I am a Bachelor
of Science in Mining Engineering. From that moment
until graduation, I completely forgot that I had not
always, from my earliest youth, intended to become
a mining engineer. Every day offered fresh reason for
forgetting. I was awfully busy for the next three years,
up to my neck in mechanics and drafting and calculus.
It was enough to make any girl forget a little thing
like Art.

One afternoon soon after my argument with Shorey,

I attended my first class in surveying. We met indoors to get our instructions. I sat on a separate bench a little way off from the men, and none of them looked at me. The instructor, too, avoided my eye in a sulky manner. He explained, with chalk on a blackboard, the simple rules for running a line with a hand level. Then he announced, "We will now go to the instrument room and take out our equipment. You people choose your partners for the term—surveyors always work in pairs. Go ahead and divide yourselves up."

He leaned back in his chair behind the desk. There were fourteen men in the class, and in two minutes there were seven couples. While the other students got up and scrambled to make their arrangements, I just sat still, wondering where I went from there.

"Well," said the instructor, "let's go and get our instruments."

We straggled after him and waited as he unlocked the storeroom. The levels we were to use, the type called "dumpy" levels, are heavy, metallic objects on tripods. Seven men stepped up and took one apiece, and then, as the instructor hesitated, I walked over defiantly and picked up an eighth. The instructor rubbed his chin and looked at me furtively. I looked at my feet.

"Damn, I was sure we had an even number in the class," he said. "I guess Bemis has dropped out."

Fourteen men and I stood there tongue-tied, impatient to bring all this to an end. Then I noticed a tall, lanky boy, who had not been in the lecture room, leaning against the door looking on, a good-natured sneer on his freckled face. He now gathered his bones together and shambled over.

"Aw," he said gruffly, "I'll take her. What the hell!"

"Oh, there you are, Bemis. O.K.," said the instructor, loud in his relief.

Bemis picked up my level and tripod and, with his free hand, waved me toward the long rod which one man of a surveying pair always carries. "Come along," he said. "I know these things. I've already run a few, working in the summer."

He turned and started to walk out, and after a second, during which I stared at him registering eternal devotion, I scampered after him. Behind me there was a loud general exhalation of relief and wonder.

Reginald Bemis—for Reginald was his name—found out all too soon that his responsibility was not temporary. Whatever whimsical impulse of kindliness had pushed him into his offer vanished when he realized that he was stuck with me for the term. But once he learned this bitter fact, he decided at least to bring me up the way I should go. He had worked in open-pit mines before coming to the university, and it was typical of his scornful attitude, that of a veteran miner, that he hadn't deigned to come to the explanatory lecture.

He was one of those gangling, undernourished boys who work their way through college; he waited on table at a hash house when he wasn't in class, and got good marks and had a future. As a surveyor, he knew his business as well as our instructor did. By the time we graduated from the dumpy level to the transit, Reginald and I had the best record of any pair of engineers for our reports and drawings. None of this excellence, obviously, was due to my talents.

Not that I didn't do my share of the heavy work. I did. We took turns carrying the cumbersome instruments. Sometimes our trail led us to a very public spot, and when passers-by suddenly noticed that I was a female—that took a moment or two, for I wore khaki coveralls most of the time—Reginald became very touchy. The minute a stranger paused to take another look at me holding up the rod or squinting laboriously into the transit, Reginald would make such ferocious noises and wiggle his fingers at his nose so insultingly that the passers-by would soon move on. His attitude was brutal but right, and I tried to show him that I appreciated it.

One evening, near the end of the surveying course, as we plodded along through snowdrifts toward the instrument room to turn in our equipment, I said to Reginald, "Excuse me for saying so, but you've been awfully nice. I don't know what I would have done that day if you hadn't said you would take me along for a partner."

"You was all there was left," said Reginald gruffly.

"Yes, but you didn't have to go on with me after that day. It must have been very hard sometimes."

"You ain't kiddin'," said Reginald, with deep feeling. "You know what they was calling me all year? Her Choice—that was it. Once I hadda fight a guy."

"It's a shame," I said. "But anyway, I've learned how
to survey."

"Oh, you ain't so dumb," he admitted. "Only trouble
with you is, sometimes you don't think straight. It's
like you was dreamin'. Like today, when we couldn't
find that bench mark. You just stood there with your
mouth open while I went around kicking snow up,
trying to find it. Lazy, that's your trouble."

"I'll try to do better," I said.

"Anyway," remarked Reginald cheerfully as we entered the door, "the worst is over. I got only one more
week with you."

"You've been *awfully* nice," I repeated.

I knew one of the geology professors socially, as it
happened, and though I never crossed his orbit in an
official way, I did drop in on him once in a while to
unburden my soul. He gave me a piece of advice early
in the game. "These boys are just afraid you'll interfere
with their daily routine," he said. "As soon as they
realize you don't, it will be all right. They've got some
idea, for instance, that they'll have to be careful of their
talk when you're around."

"You mean," I asked, brightening, "that there are
words I don't know?"

The professor ignored this and said warningly,
"Don't pay any attention, no matter what they say.
Don't expect special privileges just because you're a
woman. Try to let them forget you're a woman. Pretty
soon everything will be all right."

As a result, I trained myself to keep very quiet and

to maintain a poker face wherever I was in the college. The mining-engineering course was a stiff one, and we were all too busy to indulge in any feud, anyway. Now and then, however, some complication cropped up. I was excused permanently from one lab course because there was no ladies' room in that building.

I was also formally excused from the gymnasium classes the other coeds had to take, on the ground that I got enough exercise just learning to be an engineer. The khaki coverall garment I wore for surveying and ore dressing had to do for more orthodox classes as well, and I could see that my French teacher didn't like it, but she never complained.

It was at this time that I acquired the name Mickey as a permanent label. It was a nursery nickname of mine which had been more or less forgotten by everyone but Mother. The engineers heard it and adopted it as a more acceptable, masculine-sounding name than my real one, which was hopelessly ladylike.

Of course, there were brief flareups and resentments now and again. Some of the boys were unfair, I felt. At the beginning of a math course, one of them yelled at me, "You'll never be able to get through this! You're a girl!" Yet at the end of term, when he asked me what grade I had and I replied exultingly that I was in the first five on the list, he said, "Huh, that's just because you're a girl you got that mark." It was irritating, but after all I *had* stuck my neck out.

I continued to keep mousy quiet, and our mechanics instructor finally said to a friend, "You know, I've been dreading the day that girl would have to come to my lectures. But now that she's here, she's—why," he said in astonishment, "she's quite a lady."

As I look back on it now, I am amazed that I passed any of those examinations. Half the time and energy I should have given to my work was used up in the effort to prove that I could hold my own without being in the way. I was painfully self-conscious. My professor friend's words had sunk in so deep that I couldn't get them out of my head or my behavior. I took it as an insult when some absent-minded engineering student so far forgot himself as to hold open a door for me or stood up and offered me a chair. In time, though, most of these little frictions wore away. The one serious problem was the matter of field trips.

Field trips are study journeys into the country. Students, both of mining engineering and geology, go out with instructors and wander about looking at rock formations, geographical features, mines, or whatever they are interested in at the time.

Of course, I went out on the small trips that were over in one day, but from the longer trips, including one expedition to mines in the West, which took up a whole summer and taught the boys how to work in the tunnels, I was barred. It was simply impossible to surmount that obstacle. The Wisconsin state legislature couldn't help me this time, because the State of Montana would have kept me out of its mines. How, then, was I to qualify for my degree?

I figured something out at last as a substitute for the

mining experience. I went up that summer and stayed with relatives who had a farm in Michigan. Every morning I went out with a hand level and a Brunton compass and ran lines back and forth at half-mile intervals, straight across the township, until I had made a respectable contour map of the region to take back to the college. The authorities studied the map, smoked a few pipes over it, and unanimously voted to give it the status of the summer's field work the boys had put in.

Perhaps this really definite triumph went to my head a little. Perhaps the summer of walking alone under the Michigan sun had sweated out of me my hard-won humility. Anyway, that autumn, the beginning of my final year, I was in a mood to fight my great, all-out battle with the Geology Club.

Again, it wasn't my fault. I didn't start it; the men did. They should have known that the sign they put up on the bulletin board in Science Hall would be enough to knock me off balance. A stranger would not have understood. All the sign said, in formal lettering, was that the Geology Club was holding an extra-special meeting that night for two purposes—first, to introduce the semi-yearly crop of newcomers to the group, and, second, to hear the highly respected visitor, Professor Such-and-So, world-renowned expert on volcanoes or coral reefs or something, deliver the first of his series of lectures. But someone had added a significant line in red pencil: "Women not invited."

I recognized this as an insult aimed directly at me.
No other woman would have been crazy enough to
want to go to a Geology Club meeting. The sign was
the worse for being unnecessary. I knew perfectly well
I wasn't invited; I had not been invited, repeatedly,
for three years. They had thrashed the matter out many
times. I always pretended not to know, but it was an
old grievance, because all members of the mining-
engineering courses had heretofore automatically been
invited to become members of the Geology Club.

Once I showed up, though, the Geology Club members maintained that they were not a formal institution
of the college but a social organization, and, as such,
didn't have to abide by the cruel law of coeducation,
which forced open their lecture halls to the female sex.
True, I did belong to the Mining Engineers' Club—we
held our meetings in the ore-dressing laboratory and
cooked hamburgers in the blast furnace—but that club,
said the geologists, was different, somehow—more en-
tangled in the web of the educational setup. The geologists claimed that their taking mining engineers into
their club was a voluntary courtesy, and they said that
they preferred not to extend it to me. Inviting me
would, they said darkly, establish a precedent.

For three years I had silently accepted this argument, because I was, thank God, a lady, and besides
there didn't seem to be any way around it. This red-
pencilled message, though, affected me strongly. I was
as angry as I had been that long-ago day in the dean's
office, back in those prehistoric times when, for some

reason, I wasn't yet studying engineering.

It wasn't fair. I hadn't been bothering their old Geology Club. Yet there the men were, jeering and making faces at me in this bulletin-board announcement. Rub it in, would they? I'd show them!

My eyes narrowed as I read the sign through for the fourth time. Somebody had slipped up. Professor Such-and-So had been invited by the college faculty to give that series of lectures, and, as one of the college students, I was, of course, entitled to hear the entire series. Entitled? Why, I was probably *required* to hear them.

Not that I had ever felt any particular emotional yearning for information about volcanoes or coral reefs or whatever it was. That was not the point. The point was a matter of principle. The point was that the Geology Club, in thus selfishly arrogating one of the visiting professors' lectures to their own session, sacrificed their standing as an amateur social organization. They had made themselves, at least for the time being, one of the college classes, and that class I was entitled by law to attend. I was a perfect lady, all right, but just the same I decided to visit the Geology Club that night.

The most painfully uncertain people are the ones who seem poised and self-assured. I walked into the club meeting as bold as brass, but the slightest push would have upset me, and my old pal, the friendly professor, quite unwittingly almost administered it. As

I made my way past the rows of dismayed, silent, flummoxed men, he shouted in a whisper, "Bravo!" It took a gigantic effort to finish the walk, to sit down demurely in an empty chair, to pretend that nothing at all extraordinary was happening.

This was my first overt rebellion. Just when I had almost captured the good will of the college, too, and was so near to graduation and release. Just when they were about to confer on me the ultimate honor, the priceless boon of indifference.

The visiting lecturer saved my face, though he couldn't have known that, by climbing to the platform and breaking the tension. The ensuing hour must have gratified him, for the whole roomful of young people sat in a dead hush while he told us about volcanoes—or was it coral? If some of the graduate students hadn't been polite enough to ask a few perfunctory questions at the close of his talk, he would have noticed a strain in the atmosphere, but the amenities were properly observed, and after a vote of thanks he said good night and left us alone to wash our dirty linen.

The club president, a kindly soul named Clyde, took the floor and went through a few formalities—minutes of the last meeting and a brief résumé of the club's aims, for the benefit of the new members. Then he said, "It's our custom, just to make things less formal, to ask the men who are new to the club to introduce themselves. I'll call on them in order of seating. Mr. Blake?"

"Class of twenty-eight," mumbled a scarlet Mr.

Blake. "No other clubs. Transferred this year from Michigan College of Mines. Majoring in petrology."

Everyone grew quieter and quieter as the introductions proceeded. I wasn't just quiet; I was rigid. Were they going to pretend that I wasn't there? If Clyde skipped me, I would have to make a demonstration of some sort. I would *have* to. I held my breath until I nearly strangled. Clyde's eyes fell on me and he cleared his throat.

"Since our friend Miss Hahn has taken the bull by the horns," he said, "I will call on her to introduce herself to our new friends."

Everybody let out his breath a little; the crisis was postponed. I stumbled to my feet and duly made my recital. The meeting proceeded without interruption. Clyde finished up the official business of the meeting by announcing that it was the evening for collection of dues. If the members would kindly pay their dues—a dollar a head—to the treasurer, he said, we would be able to proceed with refreshments—the customary coffee and vanilla wafers.

We stood in line, with our dollars in our hands, and that was when the trouble started. When I reached the collection table, the treasurer shook his head. "Can't take it," he said.

"Why not?"

"Well, uh . . ." The unhappy boy swallowed hard, and then in desperation raised his voice. "Clyde! Come over here, will you?"

It had all been arranged in advance, evidently. Clyde

came over and took my arm with a sort of reluctant affection, and said, "Come on out in the hall, Mickey. I want to talk to you."

I pushed his hand away. "Talk to me here," I said.

"Come on, Mickey. Do me this favor, won't you?"

We marched out between serried ranks of embarrassed young geologists.

"It's this way," said Clyde miserably. "A bunch of us tried to—I mean, this thing came up again, the way it always does, last week, and though I personally, and some of your other friends, tried to persuade the fellows, the thing is—"

"All right," I said abruptly. "Here's my dollar, anyway. Take it for wear and tear on the bench. Nobody wants to—"

To my horror, it suddenly became urgently necessary to be alone. My unhappy nature had played me false. Whenever I am keyed up to violent anger, tears begin to flow. I ran down the hall, completely routed. This was disaster. I had committed the one unforgivable sin: I had been feminine. I wanted to kick myself for shame. I wanted to die.

What happened after that is public knowledge. Clyde walked slowly back into the clubroom and shook his head in misery when the boys asked him what had happened. "Was she awfully sore?" they asked. "Did she make a scene? Did she say—"

"Oh, gosh," said the president, "don't talk about it. She—she *cried.*"

"Cried?" Appalled, they stared at each other. Cried!

They lowered their eyes, unable to meet each other's gaze.

Somebody proposed a vote. There and then they voted.

A half hour later I was sitting in the study room at Science Hall, huddled in my chair, despair clutched round me like a blanket. There Clyde found me and brought the news. Practically unanimously, I had been elected a member of the Geology Club. One lone man who still stood out against me, admitting that his attitude spoiled the record, was yet unable to give up his convictions, and so he had left the room while the vote was taken. Public opinion had demanded that he do this.

"And in conclusion," Clyde said to me, "permit me to say that I'm sure all the fellows are *awfully* sorry it all happened."

Though stunned, I managed to say a few gracious words of acceptance, so that Clyde would leave me the sooner. I needed solitude; I had a lot of reorienting to do. I sat a long time at my desk, looking backward at a three-year program of mistaken strategy. It was the friendly professor, I realized, who had started me off on the wrong foot. Well, it was all right now. I knew better now. Just in time, too.

I blew my nose and started to search my briefcase, diving far down, trying to find a long-forgotten pocket mirror.

Margaret Sanger

There were already five children in the Higgins family when Margaret was born in 1879. Five more came after her—eleven in all. The Higginses were poor. But Margaret's mother never once questioned her so-called "natural duty" as a woman to bear one child after another—despite her own failing health and the lack of money to support the large brood.

Later, as a public-health nurse, Margaret began to question this "natural" role. She knew that too many women were dying in childbirth, some right before her eyes. She knew that it was a back-breaking burden to bear and care for so many children, leaving the woman little time or energy for a life of her own.

Margaret questioned why doctors spoke of family planning in whispers. She wondered why the Comstock Law considered the subject "obscene" and made it a federal crime to give out contraceptive information. Margaret interpreted all this as unfair—a denial of a woman's right over her own body.

In 1912 she reached a momentous decision. "It was the dawn of a new day in my life," she wrote later. "I went to bed knowing that no matter what it might cost . . . I was resolved to seek out the root of evil, to do something to change the destiny of mothers whose miseries were vast as the sky."

In 1915, Margaret Higgins Sanger published the first issue of *The Woman Rebel*, a magazine "for the advancement of women's freedom." The U.S. government banned the magazine for its mention of birth control. Margaret had many other personal setbacks, including a divorce and a self-imposed exile and a prison sentence. But she continued to work year after year to free all women from the restrictions of antiquated laws and ideas.

After twenty-four years of struggle, Margaret finally saw the Comstock Law changed, and birth control supported by the American Medical Association. The Margaret Sanger Research Bureau, a center for service, education and research in family planning, is further proof of her victory.

Margaret's father was a radical thinker of his day, and he encouraged Margaret from her earliest years to be a nonconformist. The warm bond between them weakened when Margaret's mother died and her father vented his despair in harshness toward his daughters and the young men who came calling on them.

But years later, when Margaret was organizing her campaign for birth control, her father came to her proudly and said, "Your mother would have been alive today if we had known all this then."

As the following excerpt from *An Autobiography* shows, Margaret formed and expounded her independent opinions very early in life. Her rebellion against school was set off by an unreasonably rigid eighth-grade teacher, who ridiculed her in front of the class for being two minutes late.

————————◆————————

Mother was amazed when I burst in on her. "I will never go back to that school again!" I exclaimed dramatically. "I have finished forever! I'll go to jail, I'll work, I'll starve, I'll die! But back to that school and teacher I will never go!"

As older brothers and sisters drifted home in the evening, they were as horrified as Mother. "But you have only two weeks more," they expostulated.

"I don't care if it's only an hour. I will not go back!"

When it became obvious that I would stick to my point, Mother seemed glad to have me to help her. I was thorough and strong and could get through a surprising amount of work in no time. But the rest of the family was seriously alarmed.

The next few months were filled with questions I could not answer. "What can you ever be without an education?" "Are you equipped to earn a living?" "Is factory life a pleasant prospect? If you don't go back to school, you'll surely end there."

"All right. I'll go to work!" I announced defiantly. Work, even in the factory, meant money, and money meant independence. I had no rebuttal to their arguments. I was acting on an impulse that transcended reason, and must have recognized that any explanation as to my momentous decision would sound foolish.

Then suddenly Father, Mother, my second older sister Nan, and Mary, who had been summoned to a family council, tried other tactics. I was sent for two weeks to Chautauqua, there to take courses, hear lectures from prominent speakers, listen to music. This was designed to stimulate my interest in education and dispel any idea I might have of getting a job.

My impulse had been misconstrued. I was not rebelling against education as such, but only against that particular school and that particular teacher. When fall drew near and the next session was at hand I was still reiterating that I would not go back, although I still had no answer to Nan's repeated, "What are you going to do?"

Nan was perhaps the most inspiring of all my brothers and sisters. The exact contrary to Father, she wanted us all to conform and was in tears if we did not. To her, failure in this respect showed a lack of breeding. Yet even more important than conformity was knowledge, which was the basis for all true culture. She herself wanted to write, and had received prizes for stories from *St. Nicholas* and the *Youth's Companion*. But the family was too dependent upon the earnings of the older girls, and she was obliged to postpone college and her equally ardent desire to study sculpture. She became a translator of French and German until these aspirations could be fulfilled.

At the time of my mutiny Nan was especially disturbed. "You won't be able to get anywhere without an education," she stated firmly.

She and Mary, joining forces, together looked for a school, reasonable enough for their purses, but good enough academically to prepare me for Cornell. Private education was not so expensive as today, and families of moderate means could afford it.

My sisters selected Claverack College and Hudson River Institute, about three miles from the town of Hudson in the Catskill Mountains. Here, in one of the oldest coeducational institutions in the country, the Methodist farmers of the Dutch valley enrolled their sons and daughters; unfortunately it is now gone and with it the healthy spirit it typified. One sister paid my tuition and the other bought my books and clothes. For my board and room I was to work.

Going away to school was epochal in my life. The self-contained family group was suddenly multiplied to five hundred strangers, all living and studying under one roof. The girls' dormitory was at one end, the boys' at the other, but we shared the same dining room and sat together in classes. Occasionally a boy could call on a girl in the reception hall if a teacher were present. I liked best the attitude of the teachers. They were not so much policemen as companions and friends, and their instruction was more individual and stimulating than at Corning.

I did not have money to do things the other girls did—go off for week-ends or house-parties—but waiting on table or washing dishes did not set me apart. The work was far easier than at home, and a girl was pretty well praised for doing her share. At first the students all appeared to me uninteresting and lacking in initiative. I never found the same imaginative quality I was used to in my family, but as certain ones began to stand out I discovered they had personalities of their own.

Very shortly after my arrival at Claverack I had been infected by that indefinable, nebulous quality called school spirit, and before long was happily in the thick of activities. Assembly was held in the chapel every morning, during which we all in turn had to render small speeches and essays, or recite selections of poetry. I had a vivid feeling of how things should be said, putting more dramatic fervor into certain lines than my limited experience of the theater would seem to explain, and on this account the elocution teacher encouraged me to have faith in my talents.

One vacation I announced to my family that I was

thinking of a stage career. Disapproval was evident on all sides. Father pooh-poohed; Mary alone held out hope. She said I had ability and should go to dramatic school in New York as soon as I had finished Claverack. She would apply immediately to Charles Frohman [head of an acting school] to have me understudy Maude Adams, whom I at least was said to resemble physically—small and with the same abundant red-brown hair. Lacking good features I took pride only in my thick, long braids. I used to decorate them with ribbons and admire the effect in the mirror.

The application was made.

I was photographed in various poses with and without hats. A return letter from the school management came, enclosing a form to be filled in with name, address, age, height, weight, color of hair, eyes, and skin.

But additional data were required as to the exact length of the legs, both right and left, as well as measurements of ankle, calf, knee, and thigh. I knew my proportions in a general way. Those were the days when every pack of cigarettes carried a bonus in the shape of a pictured actress, plump and well-formed. In the gymnasium the girls had compared sizes with these beauties.

But to see such personal information go coldly down on paper to be sent off to strange men was unthinkable. I had expected to have to account for the quality of my voice, for my ability to sing, to play, for grace, agility, character, and morals. Since I could not see what legs had to do with being a second Maude Adams,

I did not fill in the printed form nor send the photographs, but just put them all away, and turned to other
fields where something beside legs was to count.

Chapel never bored me. I had come to dislike ritual
in many of the churches I had visited—kneeling for
prayer, sitting for instruction, standing for praise. But
in a Methodist chapel anyone could get up and express
a conviction. Young sprouts here were thinking and
discussing the Bible, religion, and politics. Should the
individual be submerged in the state? If you had a right
to free thought as an individual, should you give it up
to the church?

We scribbled during study periods, debated in the
evenings. Without always digesting them but with
great positiveness, I carried over many of the opinions
I had heard expounded at home. To most of the boys
and girls those Saturday mornings when the more
ambitious efforts were offered represented genuine
torture. They stuttered and stammered painfully. I was
just as nervous—more so, probably. Nevertheless, I was
so ardent for suffrage, for anything which would
"emancipate" women and humanity, that I was eager
to proclaim theories of my own.

Father was still the spring from which I drank, and
I sent long letters home, getting in reply still longer
ones, filled with ammunition about the historical background of the importance of women—Helen of Troy,
Ruth, Cleopatra, Poppaea, famous queens, women au-
thors and poets.

When news spread that I was to present my essay,

"Women's Rights," the boys, following the male attitude which most people have forgotten but which
every suffragette well remembers, jeered and drew
cartoons of women wearing trousers, stiff collars, and
smoking huge cigars. Undeterred, I was spurred on to
think up new arguments. I studied and wrote as never
before, stealing away to the cemetery and standing on
the monuments over the graves. Each day in the quiet
of the dead I repeated and repeated that speech out
loud. What an essay it was!

"Votes for Women" banners were not yet flying, and
this early faint bleating of mine aroused little en-
thusiasm.

Soon I was going through the usual boy and girl
romances; each season brought a new one. I took none
of them very seriously, but adroitly combined flirta-
tiousness with the conviction that marriage was something towards which I must develop. Therefore I
turned the vague and tentative suggestions of my juvenile beaus by saying, "I would never think of jumping
into marriage without definite preparation and study
of its responsibilities." Practically no women then went
into professions. Matrimony was the only way out. It
seems ages ago.

Various pranks occurred at Claverack, such as taking
walks with boys out of bounds and going forbidden
places for tea. Towards the end of my last year I
thought up the idea that several of us should slip out
through the window and down to the village dance

hall where our special admirers would meet us. About eleven-thirty, in the midst of the gayety, in walked our principal, Mr. Flack, together with the preceptress who had come for the "ladies." We were all marched back to school, uneasy but silent.

The next morning I received a special invitation to call at The Office. I entered. Mr. Flack, a small, slight, serious, student type of man, with a large head and high brow, was standing with his back to me. I sat down. He gave me no greeting but kept on at his books. To all appearances he did not know I was there.

Then, without looking around, he said, "Miss Higgins, don't you feel rather ashamed of yourself for getting those girls into trouble last night, by taking them out and making them break the rules? They may even have to be sent home."

Although surprised that he should have known I was the one responsible, I could not deny it, but it flashed across my mind at first that someone must have told him.

He went on with rapid flow, almost as though talking to himself, "I've watched you ever since you came and I don't need to be told that you must have been the ringleader. Again and again I've noticed your influence over others. I want to call your attention to this, because I know you're going to use it in the future. You must make your choice—whether to get yourself and others into difficulty, or else guide yourself and others into constructive activities which will do you and them credit."

I do not quite recall what else he said, but I have never forgotten going out of his room that day. This could not exactly be called a turning point in my life, but from then on I realized more strongly than before that there was a something within myself which could and should be kept under my control and direction.

Long afterwards I wrote to thank Mr. Flack for his wisdom in offering guidance instead of harsh discipline. He died a few years later, and I was glad I had been able to place a rose in his hand rather than on his grave.

I spent three happy years at Claverack. The following season I decided to try my hand at teaching, then a lady-like thing to do. A position was open to me in the first grade of a new public school in southern New Jersey. The majority of the pupils—Poles, Hungarians, Swedes—could not speak English. In they came regularly.

I was beside myself to know what to do with eighty-four children who could not understand a word I said. I loved those small, black-haired and tow-headed urchins who became bored with sitting and, on their own, began stunts to entertain themselves. But I was so tired at the end of the day that I often lay down before dressing for dinner and awakened the next morning barely in time to start the routine. In very short order I became aware of the fact that teaching was not merely a job, it was a profession, and training was necessary if you were to do it well. I was not suited by temperament, and therefore had no right to this vocation.

I had been struggling for only a brief while when Father summoned me home to nurse Mother.

In an effort to be more efficient in caring for Mother I tried to find out something about consumption by borrowing medical books from the library of the local doctor, who was a friend of the family. In doing this I became so interested in medicine that I decided definitely I would study to be an M.D. When I went back for more volumes and announced my decision the doctor gave them to me, but smiled tolerantly, "You'll probably get over it."

I had been closely confined for a long time when I was invited to Buffalo for the Easter holidays to meet again one of the boys by whom I had been beaued at Claverack. Mother insisted that I needed a vacation. Mary and Nan were both there. I could stay with them, and we planned a pleasant trip to Niagara Falls for the day.

It was a folk superstition that a consumptive who survived through the month of March would live until November. Mother died on the thirty-first of the month, leaving Father desolate and inconsolable. I came flying home. The house was silent and he hardly spoke. Suddenly the stillness of the night was broken by a wailing and Toss was found with his paws on the coffin, mourning and howling—the most poignant and agonizing sound I had ever heard.

I had to take Mother's place—manage the finances, order the meals, pay the debts. There was nothing left for my clothing nor for any outside diversions. All that could be squeezed out by making this or that do had to go for shoes or necessities for the younger brothers. Mend, patch, sew as you would, there was a limit to the endurance of trousers, and new ones had to be purchased.

To add to my woes, Father seemed to me, who was sensitive to criticism, suddenly metamorphosed from a loving, gentle, benevolent parent into a most aggravating, irritating tyrant. Nobody in any fairy tale I had ever read was quite so cruel. He who had given us the world in which to roam now apparently wanted to put us behind prison bars. His unreasonableness was not directed towards the boys, who were in bed as soon as lessons were done, but towards his daughters, Ethel and me. Whatever we did was wrong. . . .

At last I realized why Father had been so different. He had been lonely for Mother, lonely for her love, and doubtless missed her ready appreciation of his own longings and misgivings. Then, too, he had always before depended on her to understand and direct us. He was probably a trifle jealous, though not consciously, because he considered jealousy an animal trait far beneath him, and refused to recognize it in himself. Nevertheless, beaus had been sidetracking the affections of his little girls. So oppressed had he been by his sense of responsibility that he had slipped in judgment and in so doing slid into the small-town rut of propriety. His belated discipline, caused by worry and anxiety, was merely an attempt to guide his children.

I, however, considered the time had passed for such guidance. I had to step forth by myself along the experimental path of adulthood. Though the immediate occasion for reading medical books had ceased with Mother's death, I had never, during these months, lost my deep conviction that perhaps she might have been saved had I had sufficient knowledge of medicine. This was linked up with my latent desire to be of service in the world. The career of a physician seemed to fulfill all my requirements. I could not at the moment see how the gap in education from Claverack to medical school was to be bridged. Nevertheless, I could at least make a start with nursing.

But Father, though he proclaimed his belief in perfect independence of thought and mind, could not approve nursing as a profession, even when I told him that some of the nicest girls were going into it.

"Well, they won't be nice long," he growled. "It's no sort of work for girls to be doing."

My argument that he himself had taught us to help other people had no effect.

Father's notions, however, were not going to divert me from my intention; no matter how peaceful the home atmosphere had become, still I had to get out and try my wings.

Althea
Gibson

Althea was all those things nice little girls are not supposed to be: rough, tough and athletic. She could fight like a champ and shoot baskets like a pro by the time she was thirteen. If she had been a boy, everyone would have considered her a daredevil. But girls are usually not praised for being big and strong—are not encouraged to compete and win. So people made fun of Althea's rugged manner and called her a "tomboy."

It hurt Althea when people made fun of her for doing what she did best and most naturally. She has this to say about her athletic ability:

"Look at her throwing that ball just like a man," they would say, and they looked at me like I was a freak. I hated them for it. I felt as though they ought to see that I didn't do the things they did because I didn't know how to, and that I showed off on the football field because throwing passes better than the varsity quarterback was a way for me to express myself, to show that there was something I was good at.

Althea never outgrew this so-called tomboy stage. Instead, she used it to advantage. Although the street kid from Harlem had to work hard to control her quick temper and her hostile attitude toward school and responsibility, she managed to develop her ability as a tennis player of the highest caliber.

In 1957, by winning the women's singles matches at Wimbledon, Althea Gibson became world champion. That day when the flashbulbs went off and reporters flocked around, Althea knew she had come a long way.

In a passage from her own story, *I Always Wanted to Be Somebody,* Althea tells about her rough childhood and about the turn of events that started her on her way to becoming a champion.

The only thing I really liked
to do was play ball. Basketball was my favorite but
any kind of ball would do. I guess the main reason why
I hated to go to school was because I couldn't see any
point in wasting all that time that I could be spending
shooting baskets in the playground.

"She was always the outdoor type," Daddy told a
reporter once. "That's why she can beat that tennis
ball like nobody's business."

If I had gone to school once in a while like I was
supposed to, Daddy wouldn't have minded my being
a tomboy at all. In fact, I'm convinced that he was
disappointed when I was born that I wasn't a boy. He
wanted a son. So he always treated me like one, right
from when I was a little tot in Carolina and we used
to shoot marbles in the dirt road, with acorns for marbles. He claims I used to beat him all the time, but
seeing that I was only three years old then, I think
he's exaggerating a little bit.

One thing he isn't exaggerating about, though, is
when he says he wanted me to be a prize fighter. He
really did. It was when I was in junior high school,
like maybe twelve or thirteen years old, and he'd been
reading a lot about professional bouts between women
boxers, sort of like the women's wrestling they have
in some parts of the country today. (Women's boxing
is illegal now but in those days it used to draw some
pretty good small-club gates.) Daddy wanted to put
me in for it. "It would have been big," he says. "You
would have been the champion of the world. You were

big and strong, and you could hit."

I know it sounds indelicate, coming from a girl, but I could fight, too. Daddy taught me the moves, and I had the right temperament for it. I was tough, I wasn't afraid of anybody, not even him. . . .

Sometimes, in a tough neighborhood, where there is no way for a kid to prove himself except by playing games and fighting, you've got to establish a record for being able to look out for yourself before they will leave you alone. If they think you're an easy mark, they will all look to build up their own reputations by beating up on you. I learned always to get in the first punch.

There was one fight I had with a big girl who sat in back of me in school. Maybe because I wasn't there very often, she made life miserable for me when I did show up. I used to wear my hair long, in pigtails, then, and she would yank on those pigtails until I thought she was going to tear my hair out by the roots. If I turned around and asked her to leave me alone, she would just pull harder the next time. So one day I told her I'd had all of that stuff I was going to take, and I'd meet her outside after school and we would see just how bad she was.

The word that there was going to be a fight spread all around the school, and by the time I walked outside that afternoon, she was standing in the playground waiting for me, and half the school was standing behind her ready to see the fun. I was scared. I wished I hadn't started the whole thing. She was a lot bigger than me, and she had the reputation of being a tough fighter. But I didn't have any choice. I had to save my face the best way I could. Anyway, my whole gang was behind me, pushing me right up to her.

We stood there for a minute or so, our faces shoved up against each other, the way kids will do, and we cursed each other, and said what we were going to do to each other. Meanwhile I tried to get myself into position, so I'd have enough leverage to get off a good punch.

She had just got through calling me a pigtailed bitch when I let her have it. I brought my right hand all the way up from the floor and smashed her right in the face with all my might. I hit her so hard she just fell like a lump. Honest to God, she was out cold. Everybody backed away from me and just stared at me, and I turned around like I was Joe Louis and walked on home. . . .

The 143rd Street block my mother and father lived on was a Police Athletic League play street, which means that the policemen put up wooden barricades at the ends of the street during the daytime and closed it to traffic so we could use it for a playground. One of the big games on the street was paddle tennis, and I was the champion of the block. In fact, I even won some medals representing 143rd Street in competition with other Harlem play streets. I still have them, too. I guess I've kept every medal or trophy I ever won anywhere.

Paddle tennis is played on a court marked off much

like a tennis court, only about half the size. You use a wooden racket instead of a gut racket, and you can play with either a sponge rubber ball or a regular tennis ball. It's a lot different from real tennis, and yet it's a lot like it, too.

There was a musician fellow, Buddy Walker, who's known now as "Harlem's Society Orchestra Leader," but who in those days didn't get much work in the summer months and filled in by working for the city as a play leader. He was watching me play paddle tennis one day, when he suddenly got the idea that I might be able to play regular tennis just as well if I got the chance. So, out of the kindness of his heart, he bought me a couple of secondhand tennis rackets for five dollars apiece and started me out hitting balls against the wall on the handball courts at Morris Park.

Buddy got very excited about how well I hit the ball, and he started telling me all about how much I would like the game and how it would be a good thing for me to become interested in it because I would meet a better class of people and have a chance to make something out of myself. He took me up to his apartment to meet his wife, Trini, and their daughter, Fern, and we all talked about it.

The next thing that happened was that Buddy took me to the Harlem River Courts at 150th Street and Seventh Avenue and had me play a couple of sets with one of his friends. He always has insisted that the way I played that day was phenomenal for a young girl with no experience, and I remember that a lot of the other players on the courts stopped their games to watch me. It was very exciting; it was a competitive sport and I am a competitive sort of person. When one of the men who saw me play that first time, a Negro schoolteacher, Juan Serrell, suggested to Buddy that he would like to try to work out some way for me to play at the Cosmopolitan Tennis Club, which he belonged to, I was more than willing. . . .

Mr. Serrell's idea was to introduce me to the members of the Cosmopolitan and have me play a few sets with the club's one-armed professional, Fred Johnson, so that everybody could see what I could do. If I looked good enough, maybe some of them would be willing to chip in to pay for a junior membership for me and to underwrite the cost of my taking lessons from Mr. Johnson. Lucky for me, that's the way it worked out. Everybody thought I looked like a real good prospect, and they took up a collection and bought me a membership.

I got a regular schedule of lessons from Mr. Johnson, and I began to learn something about the game of tennis. I already knew *how* to hit the ball but I didn't know *why*. He taught me some footwork and some court strategy, and along with that he also tried to help me improve my personal ways. He didn't like my arrogant attitude and he tried to show me why I should change.

I don't think he got too far in that department; my mind was set pretty strong. I was willing to do what he said about tennis, but I figured what I did away from the courts was none of his business. I wasn't exactly ready to start studying how to be a fine lady.

Those days, I probably would have been more at home training in Stillman's Gym than at the Cosmopolitan Club. I really wasn't the tennis type. But the polite manners of the game, that seemed so silly to me at first, gradually began to appeal to me. So did the pretty white clothes. I had trouble as a competitor because I kept wanting to fight the other player every time I started to lose a match. But I could see that certain things were expected, in fact required, in the way of behavior on a tennis court, and I made up my mind that I would go along with the program.

After a while I began to understand that you could walk out on the court like a lady, all dressed up in immaculate white, be polite to everybody, and still play like a tiger and beat the liver and lights out of the ball. I remember thinking to myself that it was kind of like a matador going into the bull ring, beautifully dressed, bowing in all directions, following the fancy rules to the letter, and all the time having nothing in mind except sticking that sword into the bull's guts and killing him as dead as hell. I probably picked up that notion from some movie I saw.

I suppose if Fred Johnson or the club members who were paying for my tennis had known the whole truth about the way I was living I wouldn't have lasted long. The Cosmopolitan members were the highest class of Harlem people and they had rigid ideas about what was socially acceptable behavior. . . .

I'm ashamed to say I was still living pretty wild. I was supposed to be looking for a job but I didn't look very hard because I was too busy playing tennis in the daytime and having fun at night. The hardest work I did, aside from practicing tennis, was to report to the Welfare ladies once a week, tell them how I was getting along, and pick up my allowance. Then I would celebrate by spending the whole day in the movies and filling myself up with a lot of cheap food.

But I guess it would have been too much to expect me to change completely right away. Actually, I realize now that every day I played tennis and got more interested in the game I was changing a little bit. I just wasn't aware of it.

Edna
Ferber

Jacob and Julia Ferber wanted their second child to be a boy—a son to carry on their proud Jewish name and someday to take over the family business. But, as Edna Ferber relates in her autobiography, *A Peculiar Treasure*, nature had something else in mind:

The doctor's tone was professionally hearty. "Well, Mrs. Ferber, you have another fine baby girl." "Girl!" shrieked the young mother in angry disappointment. "But it can't be. His name is Edward Victor Ferber. Oh, Doctor, are you sure!" He was sure. So they called her Edna.

Her father nicknamed her "Pete" from the very beginning. Pete's warm, cheerful ways soon endeared her to the father she jokingly called "Bill," and comforted him when he grew weak and blind during a long illness.

Fortunately, Edna never regretted being born a girl—and never let it stand in her way. After a brief but lively career as a newspaper reporter, she began writing short stories and then novels. Soon the stories which poured from Edna's imagination had captured the hearts of America. Her name became known in households throughout the country. *Showboat, Giant* and the Pulitzer Prize winner, *So Big,* are perhaps the best-known of her twelve novels.

The memorable characters she created were drawn straight from the lives of working men *and* women. She has the following to say about the female characters in her stories:

The major women in all my novels, plays and short stories written in these past fifty years and more have been delineated as possessed of strength, ingenuity, perception, initiative. This is because I think that woman in general—and certainly the American female of the United States—is stronger in character, more ingenious, more perceptive and more power-possessing (potentially) than the American male.

As a writer, Edna had the natural ability to project herself into any personality that interested her whether it was a waitress or a Mississippi River gambler. Her characters experienced hate, bigotry, ambition, love. Her stories brought vigor and truth to the seemingly ordinary lives of working Americans.

Edna has said that her early experience in journalism helped develop her ability as an observer of people. In the following excerpt from an early chapter of her autobiography, Edna tells of being the only woman reporter for the *Appleton Crescent.* She experienced her share of excitement, and of disappointment.

In a day when women rarely worked unless they had to, much less on newspapers, there were many "beats" Edna would not be able to cover. So when an impatient new editor fired Edna because he didn't want a woman on his staff, Edna tried to understand his position. Although she accepted this dismissal somewhat passively by today's standards, Edna was not about to give up her career. Writing was a part of her, and she spent the years to follow fulfilling her talents.

———————————————◆———————————————

There never had been a woman reporter in Appleton. The town, broad-minded though it was, put me down as definitely cuckoo. Not crazy, but strange. Big-town newspapers, such as the *Chicago Tribune* and the *Milwaukee Sentinel,* employed women on their editorial and reportorial staffs. But usually these were what is known as special or feature writers, or they conducted question-and-answer columns, advice to the lovelorn, society columns or woman's pages. But at seventeen on the *Appleton*

Crescent I found myself covering a regular news beat like any man reporter.

I often was embarrassed, sometimes frightened, frequently offended and offensive, but I enjoyed it, and knowing what I know today I wouldn't swap that year and a half of small-town newspaper reporting for any four years of college education. I'm a blank when it comes to Latin, I can't bound New York State, and I count on my fingers. But in those eighteen months I learned to read what lay behind the look that veiled people's faces, I learned how to sketch in human beings with a few rapid words, I learned to see, to observe, to remember—learned, in short, the first rules of writing. And I was the town scourge. . . .

Eight o'clock found me pounding down Morrison Street on my way to the office. Before eight-thirty the city editor had handed me my assignment sheet for the day. Dull-enough stuff, usually, for I was the least important cog in the *Crescent* office machine. When it came to news stories the city editor came first. He had his regular run—the juiciest one, of course. Next came Byron Beveridge.

All the really succulent bits fell to them—the Elks Club up above Wharton's China Store on College Avenue, where the gay blades of the town assembled; Moriarty's pool shack, the Sherman House, the city jail, the fire-engine house, the Hub Clothing Store, the coroner's office, the mayor's office, Peter Thom's stationery and tobacco store, Little's Drug Store, the Sherman Barber Shop—these were the rich cupboards from which the real food of the day's news was dispensed. There you found the facts and gossip of business, politics, scandal, petty crime.

To me fell the crumbs. They gave me the daily courthouse run and I wondered why until I discovered that it was up in the Chute at the far end of town, a good mile and a half distant. You could take the bumpy little local street car, but that cost five cents one way, and the office furnished no carfare for daily scheduled runs. Sixty cents a week was too serious a bite out of a three-dollar weekly wage. I walked it. I walked miles and miles and miles, daily. At the end of that first year my plumpness had melted almost to streamline proportions. . . .

The courthouse, the county jail up in Chute at the other end of town, these weren't nourishing news sources, but I had to cover them. Such criminals as were housed in the tree-shaded county jail were there for crimes which already had been disposed of as news. Courthouse records were made up of dry bits such as real-estate transfers in the town and the near-by farm districts. There was nothing very exhilarating about jotting down items such as "State of Wisconsin, Winnebago County, Such-and-Such Township, sixty acres northeast section, etc." But having plodded the mile and a half up there I gleaned what I could.

Bailiffs, clerks, courthouse hangers-on were a roughish tobacco-chewing crew with little enough to do. I was fair game for them. As I clattered up and down the long corridors paved with tiles, in and out of the land record office, the county clerk's office, here and there, making a lot of noise with my hurried determined step, one of the men in a group called out to me in greeting one morning, "Hi, Boots!" And Boots I remained as long as I worked on the *Appleton Crescent.* . . .

Just about this time there began to appear in the *Saturday Evening Post* a series of stories—I think by a new writer named Miriam Michelson—entitled "A Yellow Journalist." That was a new phrase; those were fresh and racy newspaper stories all about a woman reporter and her dashing adventures on a big-town paper. There was the kind of newspaper woman I wanted to be. Immediately I dramatized myself as the Girl Reporter.

Big news rarely broke in our well-conducted little town. I used to pray for a murder, but I never got an answer to prayer. In all the years of our life there, not a single murder or even a robbery of anything more than a turnip or an apple or perhaps a trinket filched from a store counter ever marred the peace of the thriving Wisconsin town. The Appletonians worked, lived, were content, behaved as civilization does when it is not frightened and resentful.

I must have been quite obnoxious but I did bring in the news. As an amateur detective in a farce gets down on his knees to examine footprints in a cracker-barrel robbery, so I made much of small events and motivations. Housewives fled at my approach, clerks dodged behind counters, policemen turned their coats inside out and hid their badges, my best friends grew wary of confidences. Life for me narrowed down to this. It was news or it was nothing. I talked to everyone—the railroad-crossing gatekeeper, the farmers in town, the interurban-car motorman. . . .

One of my duties—a hated one—was the task of getting out the society column once a week, on Saturday. To this I had to write a chatty lead, done in the butterfly manner. A search of the old *Crescent* files would here reveal some of the worst writing in the history of the newspaper profession.

Society in the formal sense bored me then as it does now. All the trite phrases of small-town society chatter of the day were tapped out on my old Oliver typewriter: ". . . leaning on the arm of her father, the bride was radiant in . . . delicate refreshments were served . . . weekly meeting of the West End Ladies Whist . . . green and white, the club colors, together with garlands of autumn flowers decorated Odd Fellows hall . . . music by Lehmann's orchestra . . . after dinner cards were played . . ."

Early in my career as society chronicler I pulled a boner. A dinner was given by Professor Plantz, president of Lawrence University, and Mrs. Plantz. I described the decorations, named the guests (mostly solemn faculty members and their wives) and then airily added, on my own, "Following dinner, cards were played."

Lawrence University was a Methodist institution, Dr. Plantz a regularly ordained minister of the Methodist

church. I was confronted next day by a battalion of
glittering eyeglasses and learned remonstrance. I suppose I looked so young and so bewildered that I was
let off with a published correction.

That taught me to make sure of my facts. Then, and
later, on the *Milwaukee Journal,* the fundamental and
unbreakable rule for reporters was the insistence on
facts, and proven facts. "It is alleged" has saved many
a publication from a libel suit, but when a statement
was made it had to be a proved statement. A reporter
who failed to verify was a reporter fired. . . .

Though my reporting job took most of my time and
energy I had enough fun of the kind an eighteen-
year-old girl should have. I was sad because I had
quarreled with my beau of high-school senior days. He
had gone off to the University of Wisconsin. Haughtily
I had asked him to return my class pin (hoping he
wouldn't). I think he felt rather embarrassed by a girl
who scouted around town for news.

Summer evenings, when young Appleton was har-
monizing "Sweet Adeline," I felt a pang of heartache.
I used to sit on the front porch in the dark, feeling
very sorry for myself (which emotion I later translated
into my first short story, "The Homely Heroine"). That
was something I was to learn by the time I turned
twenty-two: that no matter what happened to me, good
or bad, it was just so much velvet. Life really can't
utterly defeat a writer who is in love with writing, for
life itself is a writer's lover until death; fascinating,
cruel, lavish, warm, cold, treacherous, constant; the

more varied the moods the richer the experience. I've learned to value every stab of pain and disappointment. . . .

Now Meyer, the little blond city editor, left for his old job in Milwaukee, fed up with his small-town experience. He turned over to me his job as Appleton correspondent for the *Milwaukee Journal.* It became my duty to telegraph or telephone the briefest possible line on any local happening of consequence. This was called querying the paper. If they found the story of sufficient importance they would telephone or telegraph an order for the number of words they thought the story rated. Less immediate stuff I mailed in on the afternoon southbound train. Semi-feature stuff I pasted up and mailed in from time to time.

I felt enormously important and professional. Among other things the Lawrence University football games had to be covered, as well as the Ryan High School games. This was a tough assignment for a girl. It had to be caught play by play. At first I was guilty of using such feminine adjectives as "splendid" and "lovely." But after a bit I caught on to the sport writer's lingo, and I don't think that the *Milwaukee Journal* readers found the Appleton football correspondence too sissy.

Paul Hunter was the new city editor, imported from out of town, a moist, loose-hung man, eyeglassed, loquacious. He didn't like me. He didn't want a self-dramatizing Girl Reporter around the place. He began a systematic campaign. My run was cut down. My stories were slashed. My suggestions were ignored or pooh-poohed. I was in the doghouse.

Midway through my summer vacation of two weeks I got word that I needn't return. I was fired.

I can see why Hunter didn't want a girl around the place when a second man reporter could cover more varied ground. My rather embellished style of writing had no appeal for Hunter. He wanted the news and no nonsense.

The bottom had dropped right out of my world and I was left dangling in space. . . .

I had been fired just in time, but I didn't know it then. My heart was broken.

That summer I tried to interest myself in Appleton life. (As a layman. I! I who had once walked so proud as a newspaper reporter!) But the world was flat and flavorless. Eighteen years old.

In another six months I would be nineteen. Withered old age stared me in the face.

At the very nadir of this despair there appeared a message timed like a last-minute reprieve in a bad melodrama. It was from Henry Campbell, the managing editor of the *Milwaukee Journal*. He asked me to come to work on the *Journal* immediately at fifteen dollars a week, and to call him on the telephone in Milwaukee at once. In order to telephone long-distance one had to go to the main office of the telephone company.

I held the telegram in my hand. The family sat there, looking at me—my father, my mother, my sister.

There is a curiously strong bond in Jewish families.

They cling together. Jewish parents are possessive, Jewish sons and daughters are filial to the point of sentimentality. I wonder now how I ever had the courage to leave that blind invalid. It takes real courage to be selfish. Until now we had clung together, we four Ferbers. I am certain I never should have written if I had not gone.

I was wrung by an agony of pity as I looked at my father's face.

"You go on, Pete," he said. "You go if you want to."

It is lucky that youth is ruthless, or the work of the world never would be done.

I walked down to the telephone company's office and put in my call for the *Journal's* managing editor. It took some minutes to get him. As I waited in the booth, my heart beating fast, a townsman who had come into the office stood chatting with the chief operator.

"That's Ferber's girl, isn't it?"

"Yeh."

"She the one is a reporter?"

"Yeh, she's calling up Milwaukee, the *Journal* there, she says they want her to go to work for them in Milwaukee."

The other man ruminated. "Wonder a girl like that wouldn't try to do something decent, like teaching school."

Margaret Bourke-White

Photograph the inside of a steel mill? The steel-company president was baffled by Margaret's strange request. He could not understand why "a pretty young girl should want to take pictures in a dirty steel mill." So Margaret explained her fascination with the vitality of splashing hot metal and the power of machinery. She knew she could capture this hidden beauty and drama on film if given the chance.

Her intensity and determination so surprised the steel

man that he opened the doors to his mill's fumes and furnaces. Margaret went there nearly every night for a whole winter. The pioneering results were published by the once-skeptical company president in *The Story of Steel*, a booklet sent to all his stockholders.

In the years to follow, Margaret's camera was her key to world-wide adventure. After capturing the power of industry, she went on to record the starkness of rural poverty in a photo-essay, *You Have Seen Their Faces*. During World War II she became the first woman war correspondent, covering both air and ground action for *Life* magazine and for the Pentagon. Her pictures were always stark and simple, always reflecting her philosophy: "I feel that utter truth is essential, and to get that truth may take a lot of searching and long hours."

In the following passage from her autobiography, *Portrait of Myself*, Margaret tells of her unusual girlhood. Her mother kindled her curiosity and taught her to tackle things fearlessly. Her father shared with Margaret his love for experiments and inventions. No one limited her talents because she was a girl. In this way Margaret's parents helped her to face the future with courage and with confidence in herself.

———————————◆———————————

Our home was always full of creatures waiting to be born. Mother and Father were interested in natural history, and I caught that interest with such lasting ardor that it nearly made a biologist of me instead of a photographer. Mother must have been very tolerant, her sympathy for wildlife notwithstanding, to endure the avalanche of glutinous polliwog egg masses, disintegrating fragments of bark dotted with eggs of unknown vintage, and legions of moth and butterfly eggs with which I populated the house.

When Mother noticed that one of her children had developed some special interest, she had a wise way of leaving appropriate books around the house. I read the Henri Fabre classics, *The Hunting Wasps, The Life of the Grasshopper,* lived with the Comstock *Handbook of Nature Study,* which I consulted constantly as to the care and feeding of my assorted pets.

One summer I raised two hundred caterpillars under rows of overturned glasses on the dining room windowsill, brought each its favorite fresh leaf diet daily, hoping some would complete their dramatic life cycle and emerge as moths and butterflies. Only the rare ones did, but when a telltale wiggle of a chrysalis or a little rattle inside a cocoon indicated that the last splendid transformation was due, our whole family would sit up all night on the edges of our chairs to watch that magic spectacle of damp shapeless creature crawling from its shell, expanding wrinkled wings until a full-blown butterfly took form under our eyes.

Learning to do things fearlessly was considered important by both my parents. Mother had begun when I was quite tiny to help me over my childish terrors, devising simple little games to teach me not to be afraid of the dark, encouraging me to enjoy being alone instead of dreading it, as so many children and some adults do.

Father's contribution to the anti-fear crusade met with complete and unexpected success. With Father's introduction to snake lore, I decided to be a herpetologist and become so much of an expert that I would be sent on expeditions and have a chance to travel. I knew I *had* to travel. I pictured myself as the scientist (or sometimes as the helpful wife of the scientist), going to the jungle, bringing back specimens for natural history museums and "doing all the things that women never do," I used to say to myself.

Father aided my herpetology by building wire cages to house my growing menagerie of snakes and turtles. He found me a baby boa constrictor in a pet shop, nonpoisonous as are all boas, but so delicate it lived in a blanket. To Mother, such close association with the snake was doubtless new, but how could she show fear when her child was unafraid? I can still see her reading the Sunday papers in front of the fireplace— this recollection may seem odd to some readers, but to me it seems quite natural—holding in her lap my most elderly and best-behaved snake pet: a plump and harmless puff adder.

"It was her open and inquiring mind that first attracted me to your mother," my father told me years later, in what must have been a rare burst of confidence, for he was a very reticent man.

Father was the personification of the absent-minded

inventor. I ate with him in restaurants where he left
his meal untouched and drew sketches on the table-
cloth. At home he sat silent in his big chair, his
thoughts traveling, I suppose, through some intricate
mesh of gears and camshafts. If someone spoke he did
not hear.

His ink rollers and pressure cylinders traveled with
him even into his dreams. Mother, who understood him
very well (but suffered through his silence: I can still
hear her plaintive, "If only Father would *talk* more"),
kept pad and pencil always by his bedside for those
moments when he would wake for an instant, jot down
some arcs and swirls, and fall back asleep. On Sundays,
only his back was visible as he stooped over his drawing
board.

Now and then Father put the drafting tools aside
and took me with him on trips to factories where he
was supervising the setting up of his presses. One day,
in the plant in Dunellen, New Jersey, where for many
years his rotary presses were built, I saw a foundry for
the first time. I remember climbing with him to a sooty
balcony and looking down into the mysterious depths
below.

"Wait," Father said, and then in a rush the blackness
was broken by a sudden magic of flowing metal and
flying sparks. I can hardly describe my joy. To me at
that age, a foundry represented the beginning and end
of all beauty. Later when I became a photographer,
with that instinctive desire that photographers have to
show their world to others, this memory was so vivid

and so alive that it shaped the whole course of my career.

On several wonderful occasions, Father took me with him to Washington where he made a practice of investigating his own patent rights. To this day, the musty smell of filing rooms brings back the dim recesses of the old U.S. Patent Office with its towering columns of document-filled shelves and its antique white-haired attendant who, Father claimed, knew every patent by number and could produce anything needed for reference instantly without even flicking through a card file. He needed a good memory just for my father's entries, of which there were, I suppose, hundreds of basic patents concerning printing presses.

One hears that a girl falls in love first with a man who reminds her of her father. Chappie—with his gaiety, his sense of fun—was unlike my father, but when I saw him at his bench in the engineering lab, I knew here was someone who was just the same. Our dates, day or night, ended up in the lab, where Chappie showed me his latest microphotographs of wedge-shaped steel particles fused under the intense heat of his experiments and clustered in spidery patterns like Japanese silk. He believed welding would soon oust riveting on much heavy construction, and a few years later, after our paths had parted, he was to develop the special steels used on the first welded streamlined train.

Electric welding was more to him than a method,

it was a faith, and this was an attitude toward work I had met before and felt at home with. The mysterious rearrangement of molecules that went on in the burning heart of the weld was more important to Chappie than anything else in the world—except what was happening to the two of us, and that seemed bigger than the world to us both.

We chose Friday the thirteenth of June for our wedding day. We could easily have picked the fourteenth, but "to be married on Friday the thirteenth will be fun," we insisted gaily.

If there was a portent in our wedding date, there was an omen in our wedding ring also. Chappie was very clever with his hands and he decided to make the ring himself. We shopped through the jewelry stores of Ann Arbor for a gold nugget. I remember the circus had come to town that day, and we laughed when we bumped into the elephant parade every time we came out of a jewelry shop.

Everywhere jewelers tried to sell us ready-made rings, but finally we persuaded a reluctant shopkeeper to bring out a tray of accumulated gold trash, and in the midst of some cast-off gold teeth we found three small exquisite nuggets. One was the color of butter, the second almost as white as platinum, and the third gleamed up at us, a rich red-gold, asking almost audibly to be selected. It came to seven pennyweight, just right for a wedding ring.

Chappie fashioned the ring charmingly, with tiny hammer strokes making a beaten pattern over the surface. The night before our wedding he took me to the lab to give me a last fitting. He laid the lovely circle on the anvil to round it out, gave it one light tap with his tiny hammer, and our wedding ring broke into two pieces.

In two years our marriage had broken to pieces also. We were up against an age-old quandary which many brides have had to face, but few have met it with less equipment than I. As a nineteen-year-old wife, I knew, I suppose, a surprising amount about the ways of the flying fish and the butterflies, but very little of the ways of humans. I had sailed into marriage with the sun in my eyes and the wind in my hair, and when I found myself engulfed in a silver-cord entanglement, I floundered about without a compass.

"Everyone says the first year of married life is the hardest," I reminded myself. I had not expected it to be so hard as this, but surely the second year would be better. The second year was better only because we learned to face the facts more squarely and we recognized the marriage as a failure.

And now that I was facing life again as an individual, I made a great discovery. I had been through the valley of the shadow. I had lived through the loneliness and the anguish. It was as though everything that could really be hard in my life had been packed into those two short years, and nothing would ever seem so hard again. I had risen from the sickbed, walked out into the light, and found the world was green again.

People seem to take it for granted that a woman

chooses between marriage and a career as though she were the stone statue on the county courthouse, weighing one against the other in the balance in her hand. I am sure this is seldom so. Certainly in my own case there was no such deliberate choice. Had it not been for a red-gold ring that broke into two pieces, I would never have been a professional photographer.

It was sheer luck I still had that old secondhand camera when my marriage went on the rocks and I returned to college for my senior year. My mother had bought it for me when I was a freshman at Columbia and shortly after my father's death, when it was difficult for her to afford. The camera was a $3\frac{1}{4} \times 4\frac{1}{4}$ Ica Reflex, modeled like a Graflex. It cost twenty dollars and had a crack straight through the lens.

With my senior year still to go before I would get my diploma, it was a sobering thought that I had already been to six universities. It seemed that I had picked up only ill-matched smatterings of knowledge at each of them. My freshman year at Columbia I studied art, and by lucky chance took a two-hours-a-week course in photography under the late Clarence H. White, not because I wanted to take photographs but because the course dealt with design and composition as applied to photography. One doesn't learn much about photography in two hours a week, but Clarence H. White was a great teacher and the seed was planted.

At Rutgers, my second alma mater, I attended only summer school and studied swimming and aesthetic dancing. At the University of Michigan, my third, I specialized in herpetology under Dr. Alexander D. Ruthven, later the beloved president of the University.

Next, Purdue with Chappie, where I studied paleontology. Then Western Reserve night school, where I worked in the Cleveland Natural History Museum during the day.

So here I stood, with my first marriage behind me and my seventh university ahead, poring through the college catalogs. I chose Cornell, not for its excellent zoology courses but because I read there were waterfalls on the campus.

Arriving in Ithaca, I did what other college students do who are broke. I tried to get a job as a waitress. Luckily for my photographic future, the waitress jobs were all taken. By the time I got to the student library to apply for a tempting forty-cent-an-hour job there, that was snapped up too. I wept some secret tears, and turned to my camera.

I believe it was the drama of the waterfalls that first gave me the idea I should put that old cracked lens to work. Here I was in the midst of one of the most spectacular campus sites in America, with fine old ivy-covered architecture and Cayuga Lake on the horizon and those boiling columns of water thundering over the cliffs and down through the gorges. Surely there would be students who would buy photographs of scenes like these.

I knew so little about photography it seemed almost impudent to think about taking pictures to sell. All fall went into making a collection of a mere eight or ten that I felt were worth presenting. Still I was surprised at the growing feeling of rightness I had with a camera in my hands.

I arranged with a commercial photographer in Ithaca, Mr. Henry R. Head, to use his darkroom nights where I could work up sample enlargements of my pictures which he would copy "in quantity" if we ever got orders "in quantity." Mr. Head was a pillar of strength. The minuscule business he got from his end of the arrangement could never hope to balance his generous technical advice.

I belonged to the soft-focus school in those days: to be artistic, a picture must be blurry, and the exact degree of blurriness was one of the features over which I toiled during the long nights in Mr. Head's darkroom, diffusing, printing those celluloids. Ralph Steiner, whom I had met at the Clarence H. White School, a superbly sharp honest craftsman, caustically talked me into a fierce reversal of the viewpoint that a photograph should imitate a painting.

Shortly before Christmas, when I opened my little sales stand outside the dining hall in Prudence Risley Dormitory, my pictures on display looked as much like Corots as my old cracked camera plus some sheets of celluloid had been able to make them. And if I heard some admiring student murmur, "Why, these don't look like photographs at all," I took it as a high compliment.

The pictures went like a blaze. I organized a staff

of student salesmen on a commission basis to help me handle them, prevailed on the College Co-op to carry them, and then made a mistake that nearly prejudiced me against photography forever. Not realizing that the demand was seasonal, I overstocked, and tied up my small capital in print stocks which had no hope of selling for months to come. I grew to hate the sight of those pseudo-Corots piled behind my cot in the dormitory.

Five dollars came in regularly from sales for covers to the *Alumni News.* I began getting letters from alumni of Cornell who were architects, inquiring whether I intended to go into photography after I got out of school, and stating there were few good architectural photographers in the country.

This opened a dazzling new vista. Never had I thought of becoming a professional photographer. Also it opened a new conflict. Should I drop my biology for a field for which I was so little trained? On the biology side I had something that looked pretty close to an offer from the Curator of Herpetology at the Museum of Natural History in New York. But to be a professional photographer—what a tantalizing possibility!

I must get an unbiased opinion of my work, I told myself. These architects were graduates of Cornell after all, bound to be sentimental about pictures of their alma mater. I would go to New York during Easter vacation, walk in on some architect cold, and base my momentous decision on his opinion.

Someone gave me the name of York & Sawyer, a large architectural firm, and suggested asking for Mr. Benjamin Moskowitz. Arriving unwisely late in the day, I went into the upper reaches of the New York Central Office Building, entered a frighteningly spacious lobby, and asked to see Mr. Moskowitz.

The tall dark man who came out in response to this request was plainly a commuter on his way to the train. As I outlined my problem, he was unobtrusively though steadily edging his way toward the elevator. I did not realize he had not taken in a word when he pushed the down button, but I was chilled by the lack of response. If the elevator had arrived immediately, I am sure that the next morning would have found me on the doorstep of the Museum of Natural History. But as we waited, the silence became so embarrassing that I opened my big portfolio. Mr. Moskowitz glanced at the picture on top, a view of the library tower.

"Did you take this photograph?"

"Yes, that's what I've been telling you."

"Did you take it yourself?"

I repeated my little tale, how I was considering becoming an architectural photographer, but first I wanted the unbiased opinion of an architect as to whether I had the ability for the work.

"Let's go back into the office and look at these," said the unpredictable Mr. Moskowitz.

He let his train go, stood up the photographs against the dark wood paneling of the conference room and called in the other members of the firm to look them over. After the kind of golden hour one remembers for a lifetime, I left with the assurance of Messrs. York, Sawyer, and associates that I could "walk into any architect's office in the country with that portfolio and get work."

Everything was touched with magic now. The Cornell pictures, both the blurry and the in-focus ones, sold out in the commencement rush. College over, I took the Great Lakes night boat from Buffalo to Cleveland, and rising early, I stood on the deck to watch the city come into view. As the skyline took form in the early morning mist, I felt I was coming to my promised land: columns of masonry gaining height as we drew toward the pier, derricks swinging like living creatures—deep inside I knew these were my subjects.

One personal task remained to be completed. Cleveland was my legal "place of residence"—that was why I had returned to it. On a rainy Saturday morning I slipped down to the courthouse, quietly got my divorce, and resumed my maiden name. I used my full name, with the addition of a hyphen. Bourke had been my mother's choice for my middle name, and she always liked me to use it in full.

I had closed the room; I had come out whole and happy with the knowledge of my new strength, and nothing would ever seem hard to me again. I was embarked on my new life.

Bibliography

The books from which selections were taken for this
anthology are available in the following editions:

Don't Fall Off the Mountain by Shirley MacLaine. Hardcover:
W. W. Norton and Company. Paperback: Bantam Books.

Unbought and Unbossed by Shirley Chisholm. Hardcover: Houghton Mifflin Company.

The Long Loneliness by Dorothy Day. Hardcover: Harper and
Row, Publishers.

Times and Places by Emily Hahn. Hardcover: T. Y. Crowell
Company.

An Autobiography by Margaret Sanger. Hardcover: W. W. Norton and Company. (Although this edition has gone out of print,
it is available in some libraries.)

I Always Wanted to Be Somebody by Althea Gibson. Hardcover:
Harper and Row, Publishers. Paperback: Perennial Library, Harper
and Row, Publishers. Special paperback abridgment: Falcon
Books, Noble and Noble Publishers, Dell Publishing Company.

A Peculiar Treasure by Edna Ferber. Hardcover: Doubleday and
Company. Paperback: Lancer Books.

Portrait of Myself by Margaret Bourke-White. Hardcover: Simon
and Schuster.

Pat Ross *is a free-lance writer and an editor of books
for young readers at Alfred A. Knopf, Inc. Formerly she
was managing editor of* Humpty Dumpty's Magazine.
*An active member of Feminists on Children's Media, she
coordinated the group's booklet of non-sexist titles re-
commended for young readers,* Little Miss Muffet Fights
Back.

*Raised in Chestertown, Maryland, she received a degree
in early childhood education from Hood College. She and
her husband, Joel, enjoy travel and skiing.*

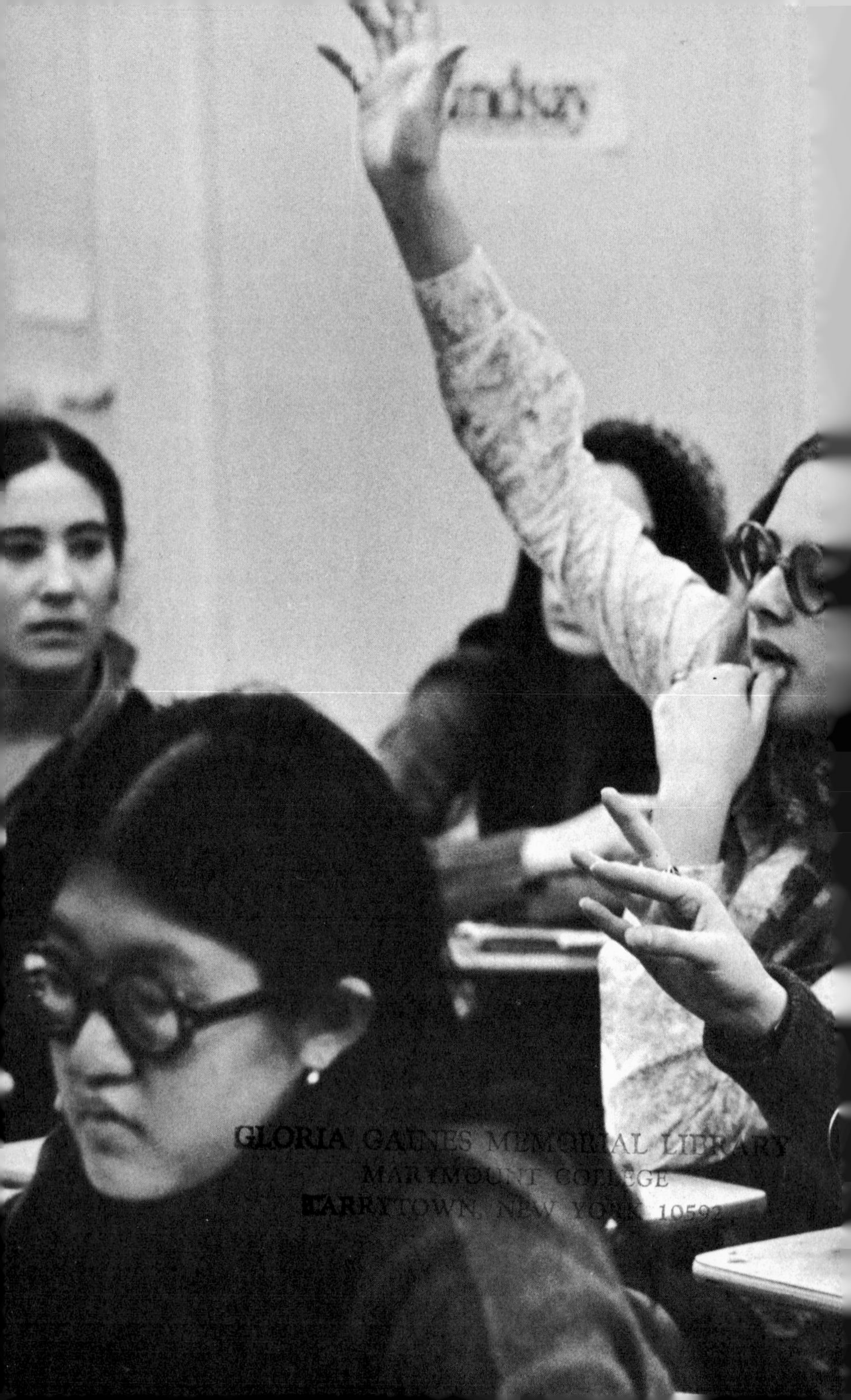
Monday